MENSA
PUBLICATIONS

NUMBER PUZZLES

FOR MATH GENIUSES

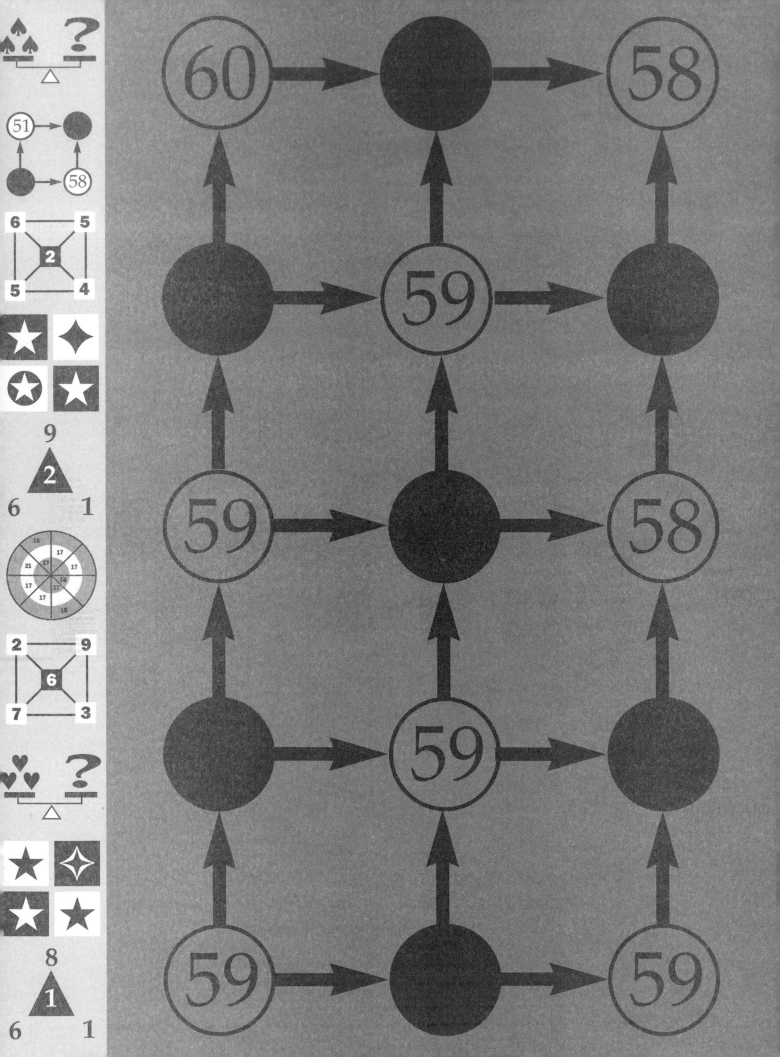

NUMBER PUZZLES

FOR MATH GENIUSES

HAROLD GALE

TIMES
BOOKS

INTRODUCTION

PUZZLES using numbers have become more and more popular over the years. Some of the puzzles are purely mathematical and involve the use of simple processes. There are others, however, which although appearing to use one branch of mathematics can be solved more easily and quickly by using a little logical thought. Before attempting a puzzle, consider it very carefully and quite often the solution stands out clearly.

One main aid in the production of number puzzles is the computer. Once a program has been written, puzzles can be generated at a very fast rate. However, this does not dispense with the need for other human assistance.

Fortunately I have an extremely able helper in Carolyn Skitt. She checks, criticizes and improves on many of the puzzles produced. Without Carolyn this book would still be in the making. Help has also come from other quarters. Joanne Harris spent a great deal of time perfecting the tinted puzzles, Bobby Raikhy worked on the many diagrammatic styles, and David Ballheimer checked the proofs. But what of Mensa?

If you can solve the puzzles, can you join the organization? You should have no problem. These are fun puzzles but they are by no means easy. If you can work these out, the Mensa test should prove to be no hurdle and you should easily qualify. Once you have joined you will find a feeling of self-satisfaction that very few experience in a lifetime. You will meet people of different walks of life but of similar brainpower. A scientist can meet a poet, a composer, or an architect. The broadening of the intellectual vision is amazing. The new horizon is formidable, but challenging. I invite you to join this ever-expanding group of people, where race, religion or political persuasion are no blocks but keys: keys to opening new doors of understanding, friendship and considered discussion.

There are over 50,000 Mensa members in the USA alone and over 120,000 throughout the world. Write to: American Mensa Inc., 2626 East 14th Street, Brooklyn, NY 11235-3992.

HAROLD GALE
Chief Executive of Mensa Publications
March, 1993.

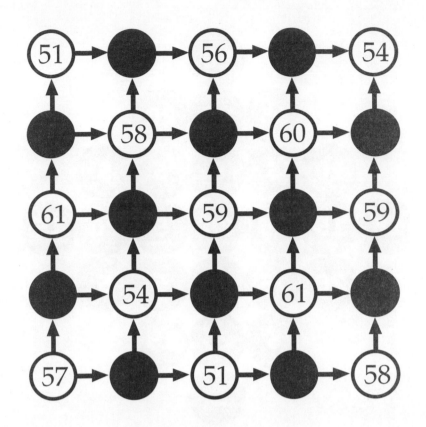

NUMBER PUZZLE 1

Move from the bottom left-hand corner to the top right-hand
corner following the arrows. Add the numbers on your route
together. If each black spot is worth minus 23,
how many different routes are there to score 188?

ANSWER 62

NUMBER PUZZLE 2

Place the tiles in a square to give some five-figure numbers.
When this has been done accurately the same
five numbers can be read both down and across.
How does the finished square look?

ANSWER 10

NUMBER PUZZLE 3

Start in the middle circle and move from circle to touching circle.
Collect the four numbers which will total 70. Once a route has
been found return to the middle circle and start again.
If a route can be found, which obeys the above rules but follows
both a clockwise and an anticlockwise path, it is treated as two
different routes.
How many different ways are there?

ANSWER 103

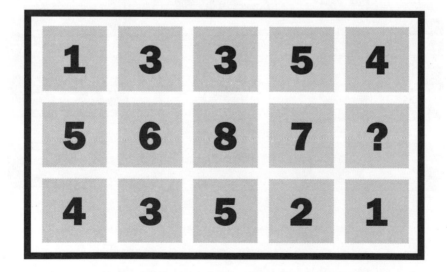

NUMBER PUZZLE 4

Which number should replace the question mark in the diagram?

ANSWER 51

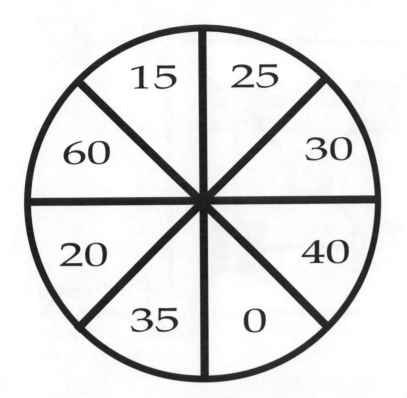

NUMBER PUZZLE 5

You have four shots with each go to score 75. Aim at this target and work out how many different ways there are to make the score. Assume each shot scores and once four numbers have been used the same four cannot be used again in another order.
How many are there?

ANSWER 92

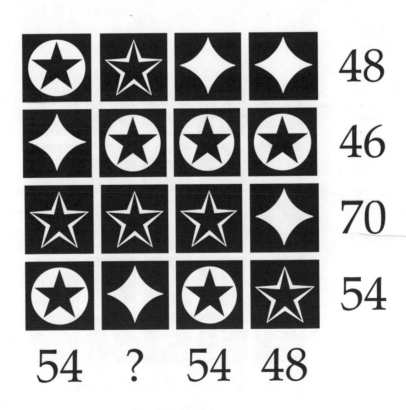

NUMBER PUZZLE 6

The contents of each box has a value. The total of the values is shown alongside a row or beneath a column. Which number should replace the question mark?

ANSWER 40

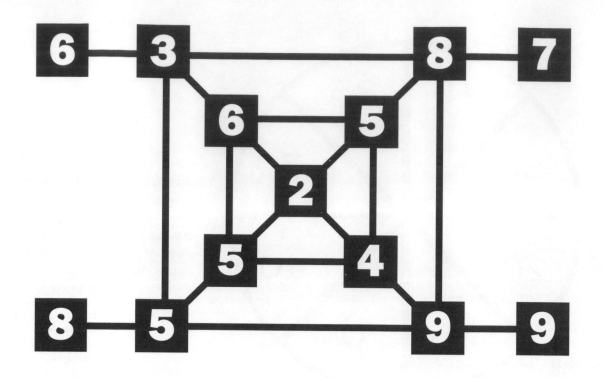

NUMBER PUZZLE 7

Start at any corner number and collect another four numbers by
following the paths shown. Add the five numbers together.
What is the highest total which can be attained?

ANSWER 82

NUMBER PUZZLE 8

Move from square to adjacent square either vertically or horizontally. Begin at the bottom left-hand square and end at the top right-
hand square. Collect nine numbers and total them. How many
different ways are there to total 38?

ANSWER 30

A B C D E

6	3	3	9	6
5	4	1	9	8
7	1	6	8	
8	1	7	9	
4	3	1	7	6

NUMBER PUZZLE 9

There is a relationship between the columns of numbers in this diagram. The letters above the grid are there to help you. Which number should be placed in the empty squares?

ANSWER 72

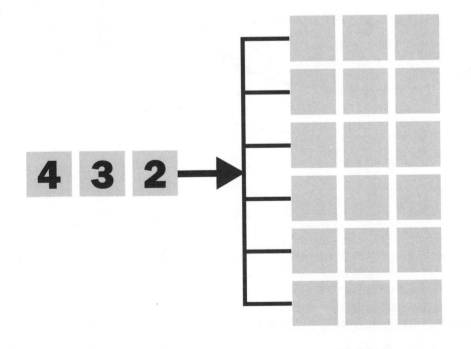

NUMBER PUZZLE 10

Place six three digit numbers of 100 plus at the end of 432 so that six numbers of six digits are produced. When each number is divided by 151 six whole numbers can be found. Which numbers should be placed in the grid?

ANSWER 20

NUMBER PUZZLE 11

Each row, column and five-figure diagonal line
in this diagram must total 85. Four different numbers must be
used, as many times as necessary, to achieve this.
What are the numbers?

ANSWER 61

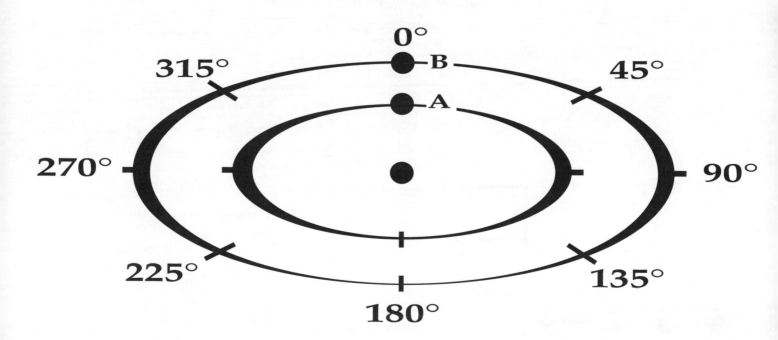

NUMBER PUZZLE 12

Two planets are in line with each other and the sun.
The outer planet will orbit the sun every twelve years. The inner
planet takes three years. Both move in a clockwise direction.
When will they next form a straight line with each other and the
sun? The diagram should help you.

ANSWER 9

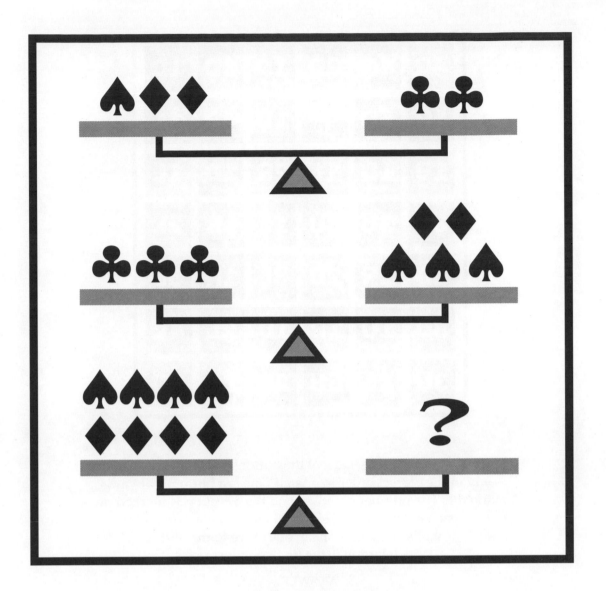

NUMBER PUZZLE 13

The top two scales are in perfect balance.
How many clubs will be needed to balance the bottom set?

ANSWER 102

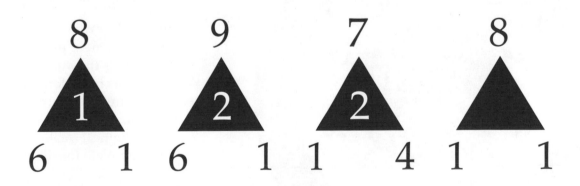

NUMBER PUZZLE 14

Which figure should be placed in the empty triangle?

ANSWER 50

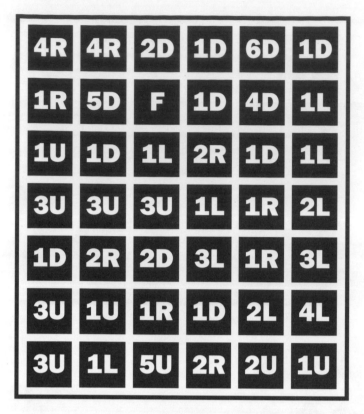

NUMBER PUZZLE 15

Here is an unusual safe. Each of the buttons must be pressed once
only in the correct order to open it. The last button is always
marked F. The number of moves and the direction is marked on
each button. Thus 1U would mean one move up
whilst 1L would mean one move to the left.
Which button is the first you must press.

ANSWER 91

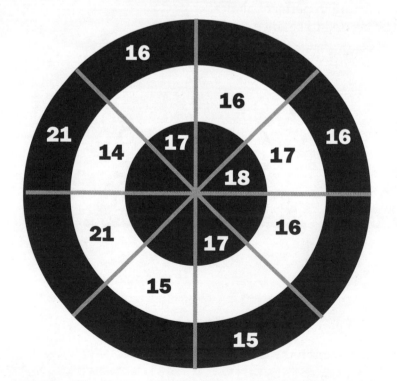

NUMBER PUZZLE 16

Complete the grid in such a way
that each segment of three numbers
totals the same.
When this has been done correctly
each of the three concentric circles of
eight numbers will produce three
identical totals.
Now complete the diagram.

ANSWER 39

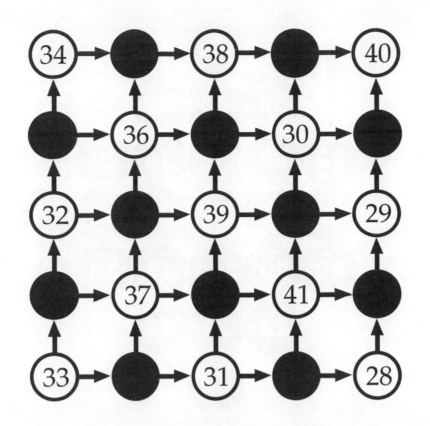

NUMBER PUZZLE 17

Move from the bottom left-hand corner to the top right-hand
corner following the arrows. Add the numbers on your route
together. If each black spot is worth minus 8,
how many different routes are there to score 155?

ANSWER 81

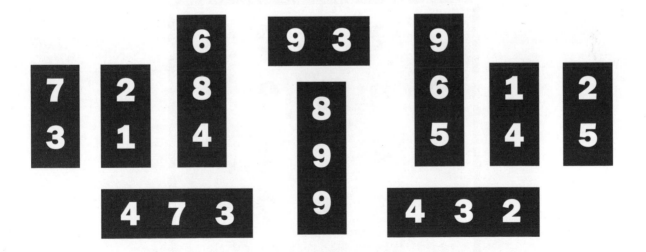

NUMBER PUZZLE 18

Place the tiles in a square to give some five-figure numbers. When
this has been done accurately the same
five numbers can be read both down and across.
How does the finished square look?

ANSWER 29

NUMBER PUZZLE 19

Start in the middle circle and move from circle to touching circle.
Collect the four numbers which will total 70. Once a route has
been found return to the middle circle and start again.
If a route can be found, which obeys the above rules but follows
both a clockwise and an anti-clockwise path, it is treated as two
different routes. How many different ways are there?

ANSWER 71

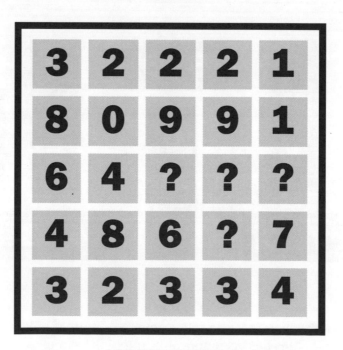

NUMBER PUZZLE 20

Which number should replace the question marks in the diagram?

ANSWER 19

NUMBER PUZZLE 21

You have four shots with each go to score 51. Aim at this target and work out how many different ways there are to make the score. Assume each shot scores and once four numbers have been used the same four cannot be used again in another order.
How many are there?

ANSWER 8

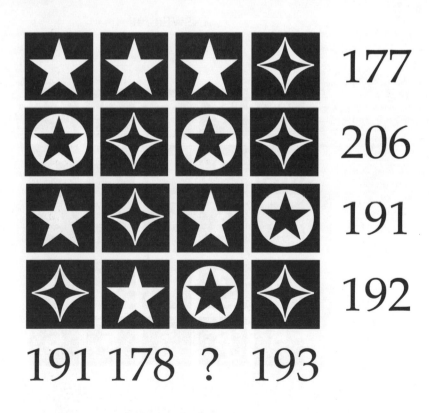

177

206

191

192

191 178 ? 193

NUMBER PUZZLE 22

The contents of each box has a value. The total of the values is shown alongside a row or beneath a column. Which number should replace the question mark?

ANSWER 60

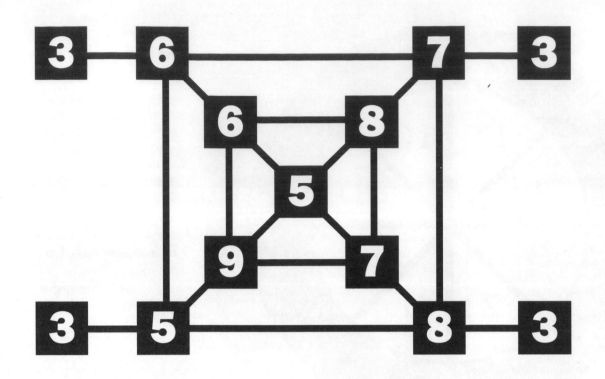

NUMBER PUZZLE 23

Start at any corner number and collect another four numbers by
following the paths shown. Add the five numbers together.
How many times can you score 27?

ANSWER 101

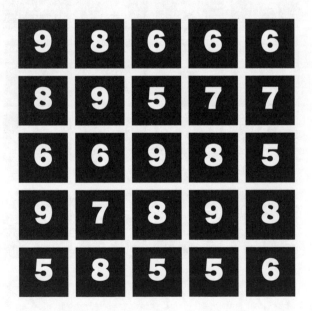

NUMBER PUZZLE 24

Move from square to adjacent square either vertically or horizontally. Begin at the bottom left-hand square and end at the top right-
hand square. Collect nine numbers and total them. How many
different ways are there to total 66?

ANSWER 49

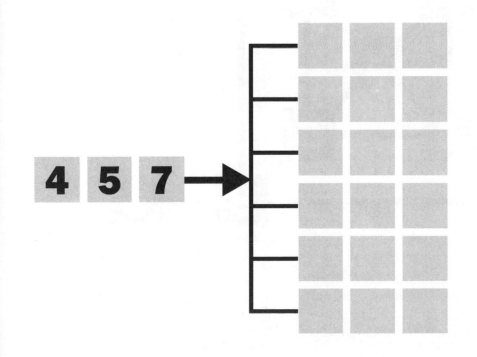

A B C D E

A	B	C	D	E
8	2	8	6	4
9	4	7	5	1
9	3	8	6	
7	1	8	6	5
7	2	7	5	

NUMBER PUZZLE 25

There is a relationship between the columns of numbers in this diagram. The letters above the grid are there to help you. Which number should be placed in the empty squares?

ANSWER 90

4 5 7 →

NUMBER PUZZLE 26

Place six three digit numbers of 100 plus at the end of 457 so that six numbers of six digits are produced. When each number is divided by 55.5 six whole numbers can be found. Which numbers should be placed in the grid?

ANSWER 38

19		22	6	
9		23	20	7
20		16		
		9		27
	14	10	32	13

NUMBER PUZZLE 27

Each row, column and five-figure diagonal line
in this diagram must total 80. Three different numbers must be
used, as many times as necessary, to achieve this.
What are the numbers?

ANSWER 80

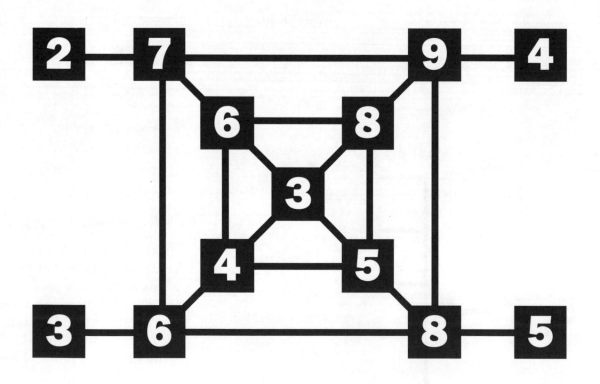

NUMBER PUZZLE 28

Start at the corner number and collect another four numbers by
following the paths shown. Add the five numbers together.
How many times can you score 24?

ANSWER 28

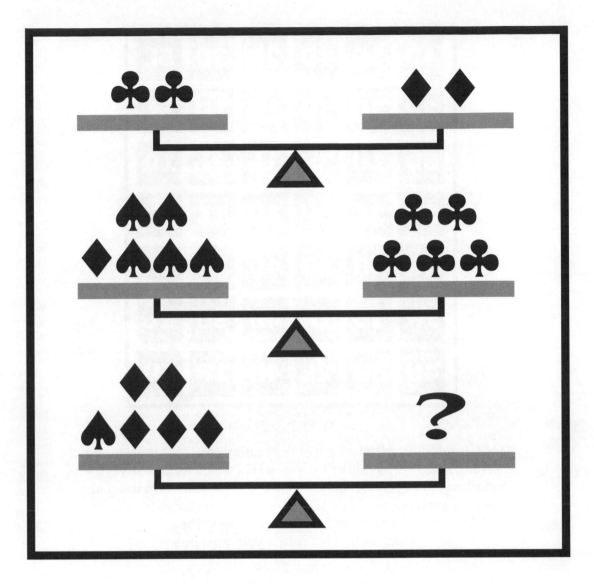

NUMBER PUZZLE 29

The top two scales are in perfect balance.
How many clubs will be needed to balance the bottom set?

ANSWER 70

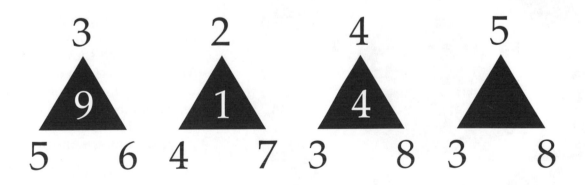

NUMBER PUZZLE 30

Which figure should be placed in the empty triangle?

ANSWER 18

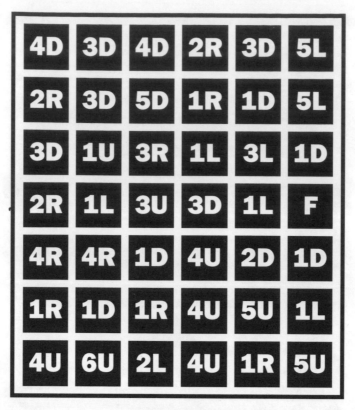

4D	3D	4D	2R	3D	5L
2R	3D	5D	1R	1D	5L
3D	1U	3R	1L	3L	1D
2R	1L	3U	3D	1L	F
4R	4R	1D	4U	2D	1D
1R	1D	1R	4U	5U	1L
4U	6U	2L	4U	1R	5U

NUMBER PUZZLE 31

Here is an unusual safe. Each of the buttons must be pressed once
only in the correct order to open it. The last button is always
marked F. The number of moves and the direction is marked on
each button. Thus 1U would mean one move up
whilst 1L would mean one move to the left.
Which button is the first you must press.

ANSWER 59

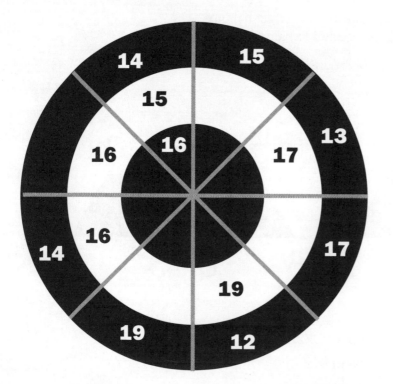

NUMBER PUZZLE 32

Complete the grid in such a way
that each segment of three numbers
totals the same.
When this has been done correctly
each of the three concentric circles of
eight numbers will produce three
identical totals.
Now complete the diagram.

ANSWER 7

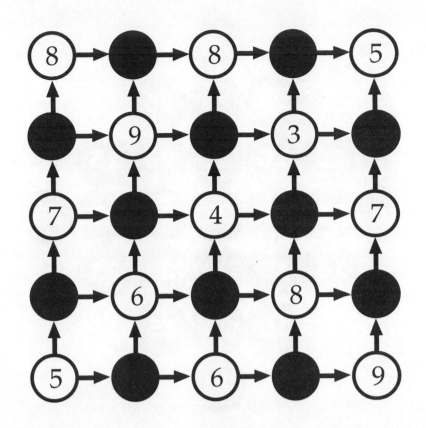

NUMBER PUZZLE 33

Move from the bottom left-hand corner to the top right-hand
corner following the arrows. Add the numbers on your route
together. If each black spot is worth 2,
how many different routes are there to score 40?

ANSWER 100

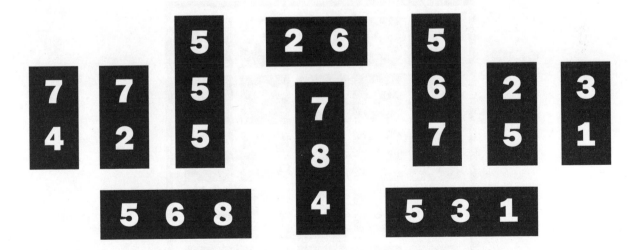

NUMBER PUZZLE 34

Place the tiles in a square to give some five-figure numbers. When
this has been done accurately the same
five numbers can be read both down and across.
How does the finished square look?

ANSWER 48

NUMBER PUZZLE 35

Start in the middle circle and move from circle to touching circle.
Collect the four numbers which will total 90. Once a route has
been found return to the middle circle and start again.
If a route can be found, which obeys the above rules but follows
both a clockwise and an anticlockwise path, it is treated as two
different routes. How many different ways are there?

ANSWER 89

NUMBER PUZZLE 36

Which number should replace the question mark in the diagram?

ANSWER 37

NUMBER PUZZLE 37

You have four shots with each go to score 49. Aim at this target and work out how many different ways there are to make the score. Assume each shot scores and once four numbers have been used the same four cannot be used again in another order.
How many are there?

ANSWER 79

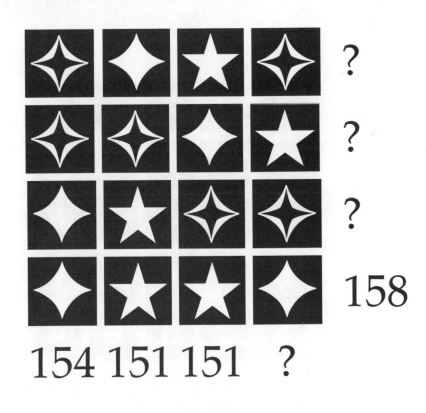

NUMBER PUZZLE 38

The contents of each box has a value. The total of the values is shown alongside a row or beneath a column. Which number should replace the question marks?

ANSWER 27

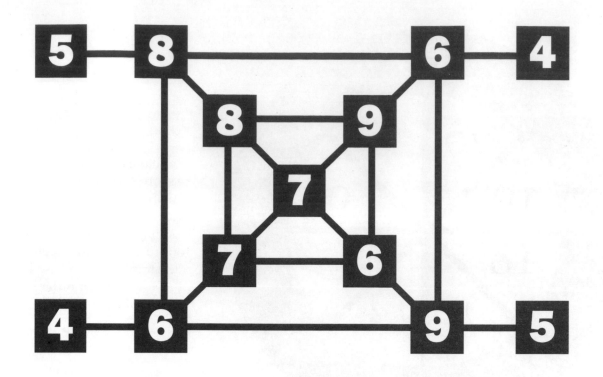

NUMBER PUZZLE 39

Start at the corner number and collect another four numbers by
following the paths shown. Add the five numbers together.
What is the lowest number you can score?

ANSWER 69

NUMBER PUZZLE 40

Move from square to adjacent square either vertically or horizontally. Begin at the bottom left-hand square and end at the top right-
hand square. Collect nine numbers and total them.
How many different ways are there to total 35?

ANSWER 17

A B C D E

A	B	C	D	E
6	1	5	7	
5	1	4	6	
4	2	2	6	4
3	2	1	5	4
4	1	3	5	

NUMBER PUZZLE 41

There is a relationship between the columns of numbers in this
diagram. The letters above the grid are there to help you.
Which number should be placed in the empty squares?

ANSWER 58

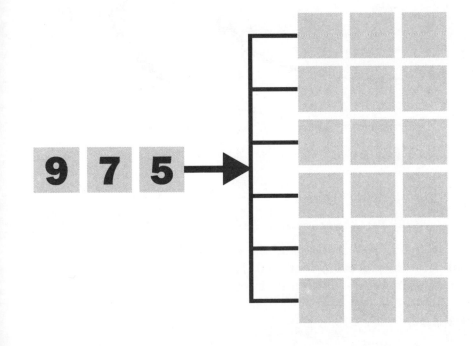

NUMBER PUZZLE 42

Place six three digit numbers of
100 plus at the end of 975 so that
six numbers of six digits are
produced. When each number is
divided by 65.5 six whole
numbers can be found. Which
numbers should be placed in
the grid?

ANSWER 6

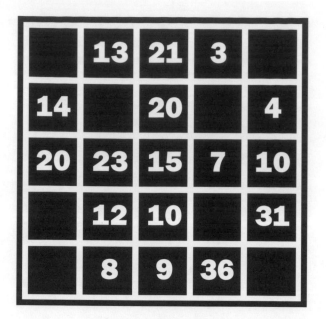

NUMBER PUZZLE 43

Each row, column and five-figure diagonal line
in this diagram must total 75. Three different numbers must be
used, as many times as necessary, to achieve this.
What are the numbers?

ANSWER 99

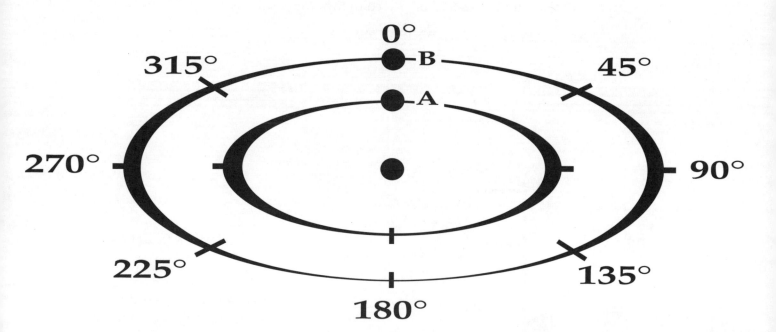

NUMBER PUZZLE 44

Two planets are in line with each other and the sun.
The outer planet will orbit the sun every six years. The inner
planet takes two years. Both move in a clockwise direction. When
will they next form a straight line with each other and the sun?
The diagram should help you.

ANSWER 47

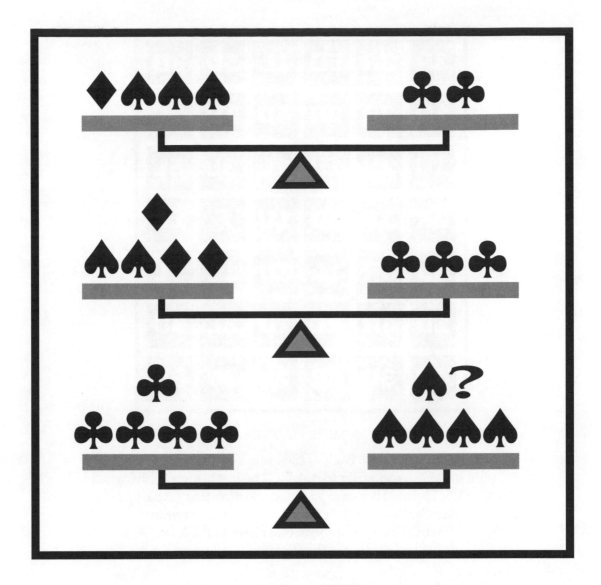

NUMBER PUZZLE 45

The top two scales are in perfect balance.
How many diamonds will be needed to balance the bottom set?

ANSWER 88

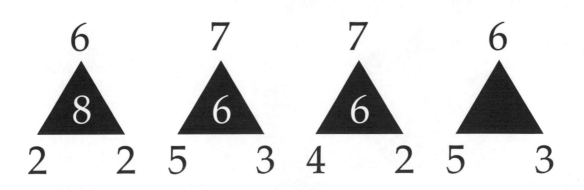

NUMBER PUZZLE 46

Which figure should be placed in the empty triangle?

ANSWER 36

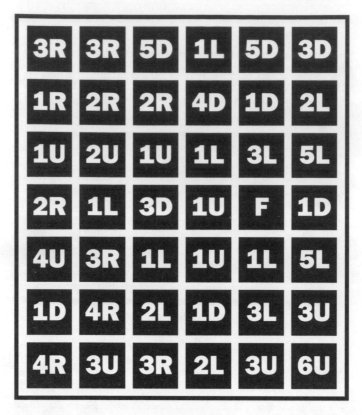

3R	3R	5D	1L	5D	3D
1R	2R	2R	4D	1D	2L
1U	2U	1U	1L	3L	5L
2R	1L	3D	1U	F	1D
4U	3R	1L	1U	1L	5L
1D	4R	2L	1D	3L	3U
4R	3U	3R	2L	3U	6U

NUMBER PUZZLE 47

Here is an unusual safe. Each of the buttons must be pressed once
only in the correct order to open it. The last button is always
marked F. The number of moves and the direction is marked on
each button. Thus 1U would mean one move up
whilst 1L would mean one move to the left.
Which button is the first you must press.

ANSWER 78

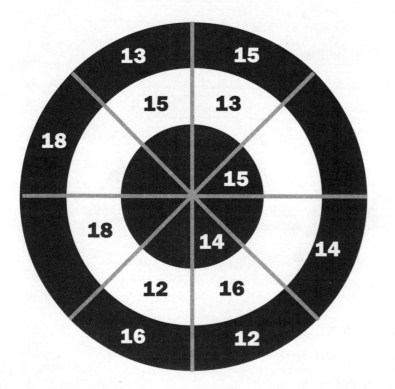

NUMBER PUZZLE 48

Complete the grid in such a way
that each segment of three numbers
totals the same.
When this has been done correctly
each of the three concentric circles of
eight numbers will produce
identical totals.
Now complete the diagram.

ANSWER 26

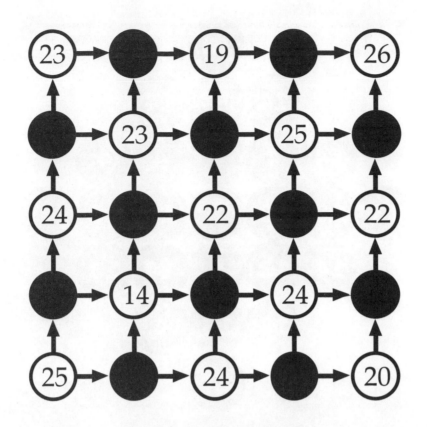

NUMBER PUZZLE 49

Move from the bottom left-hand corner to the top right-hand
corner following the arrows. Add the numbers on your route
together. If each black spot is worth minus 13,
how many different routes are there to score 69?

ANSWER 68

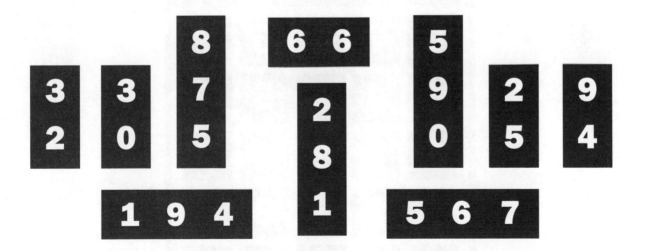

NUMBER PUZZLE 50

Place the tiles in a square to give some five-figure numbers. When
this has been done accurately the same
five numbers can be read both down and across.
How does the finished square look?

ANSWER 16

NUMBER PUZZLE 51

Start in the middle circle and move from circle to touching circle.
Collect the four numbers which will total 42. Once a route has
been found return to the middle circle and start again.
If a route can be found, which obeys the above rules but follows
both a clockwise and an anticlockwise path, it is treated as two
different routes. How many different ways are there?

ANSWER 57

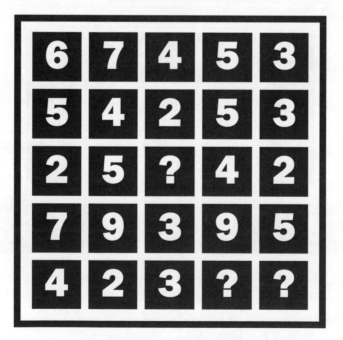

NUMBER PUZZLE 52

Which number should replace the question marks in the diagram?

ANSWER 5

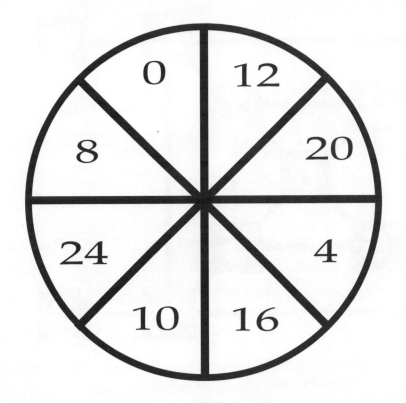

NUMBER PUZZLE 53

You have four shots with each go to score 48. Aim at this target and work out how many different ways there are to make the score. Assume each shot scores and once four numbers have been used the same four cannot be used again in another order.
How many are there?

ANSWER 98

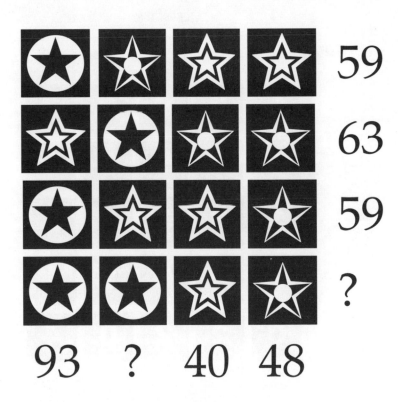

NUMBER PUZZLE 54

The contents of each box has a value. The total of the values is shown alongside a row or beneath a column. Which number should replace the question marks?

ANSWER 46

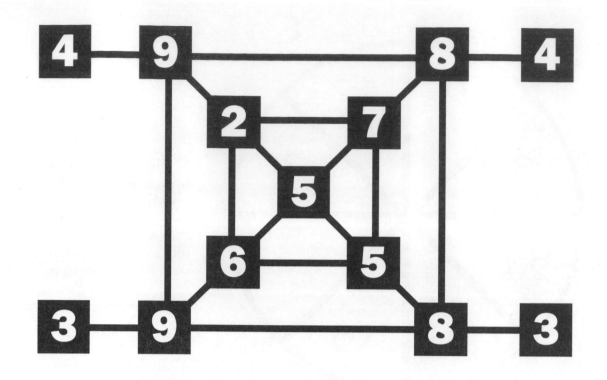

NUMBER PUZZLE 55

Start at any corner number and collect another four numbers by following the paths shown. Add the five numbers together. How many times can you score 29?

ANSWER 87

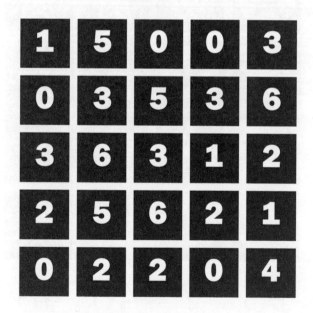

NUMBER PUZZLE 56

Move from square to adjacent square either vertically or horizontally. Begin at the bottom left-hand square and end at the top right-hand square. Collect nine numbers and total them. How many different ways are there to total 30?

ANSWER 35

A	B	C	D	E
8	0	8	9	8
5	4	1	2	5
6	2	4	5	6
4	1	3	4	
3	2	1	2	3

NUMBER PUZZLE 57

There is a relationship between the columns of numbers in this diagram. The letters above the grid are there to help you. Which number should be placed in the empty squares?

ANSWER 77

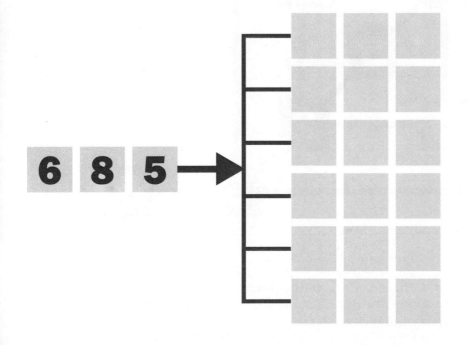

NUMBER PUZZLE 58

Place six three digit numbers of 100 plus at the end of 685 so that six numbers of six digits are produced. When each number is divided by 111 six whole numbers can be found. Which numbers should be placed in the grid?

ANSWER 25

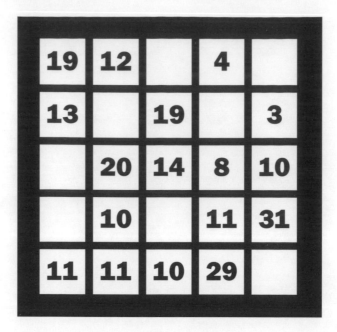

NUMBER PUZZLE 59

Each row, column and five-figure diagonal line
in this diagram must total 70. Three different numbers must be
used, as many times as necessary, to achieve this.
What are the numbers?

ANSWER 67

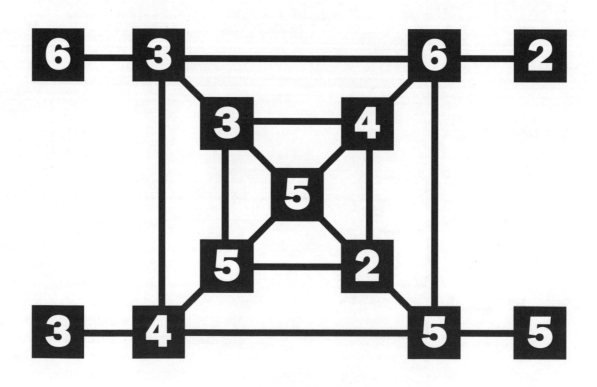

NUMBER PUZZLE 60

Start at the corner number and collect another four numbers by
following the paths shown. Add the five numbers together.
How many times can you score 17?

ANSWER 15

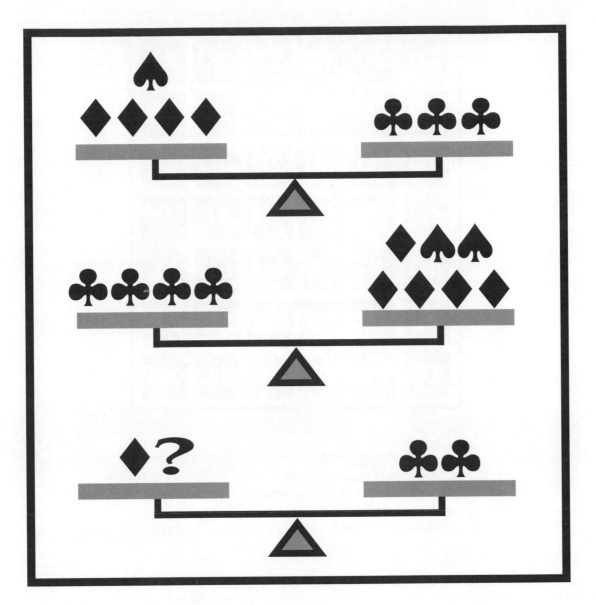

NUMBER PUZZLE 61

The top two scales are in perfect balance.
How many spades will be needed to balance the bottom set?

ANSWER 56

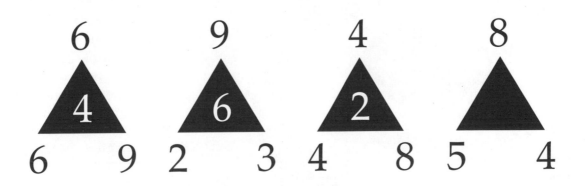

NUMBER PUZZLE 62

Which figure should be placed in the empty triangle?

ANSWER 4

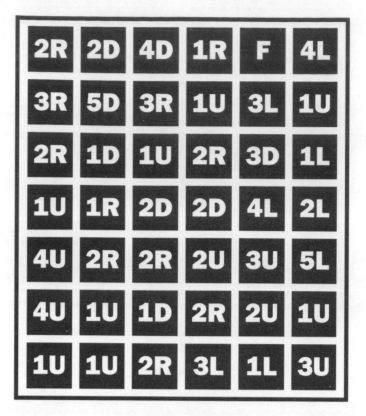

2R	2D	4D	1R	F	4L
3R	5D	3R	1U	3L	1U
2R	1D	1U	2R	3D	1L
1U	1R	2D	2D	4L	2L
4U	2R	2R	2U	3U	5L
4U	1U	1D	2R	2U	1U
1U	1U	2R	3L	1L	3U

NUMBER PUZZLE 63

Here is an unusual safe. Each of the buttons must be pressed once
only in the correct order to open it. The last button is always
marked F. The number of moves and the direction is marked on
each button. Thus 1U would mean one move up
whilst 1L would mean one move to the left.
Which button is the first you must press.

ANSWER 97

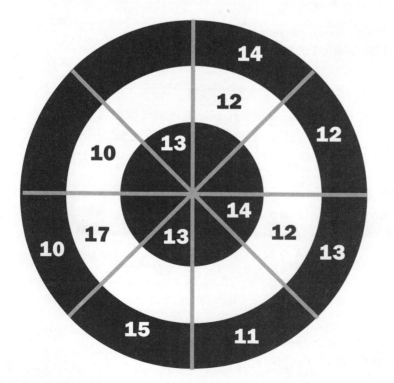

NUMBER PUZZLE 64

Complete the grid in such a way
that each segment of three numbers
totals the same.
When this has been done correctly
each of the three concentric circles of
eight numbers will produce
identical totals.
Now complete the diagram.

ANSWER 45

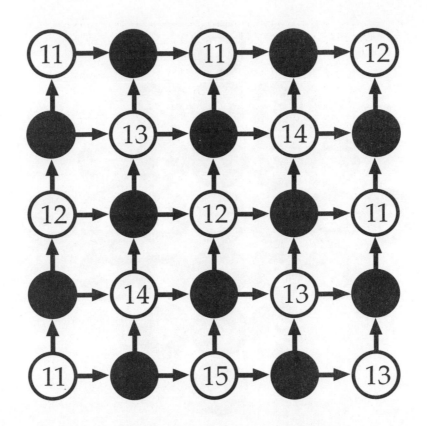

NUMBER PUZZLE 65

Move from the bottom left-hand corner to the top right-hand
corner following the arrows. Add the numbers on your route
together. If each black spot is worth 9,
how many different routes are there to score 94?

ANSWER 86

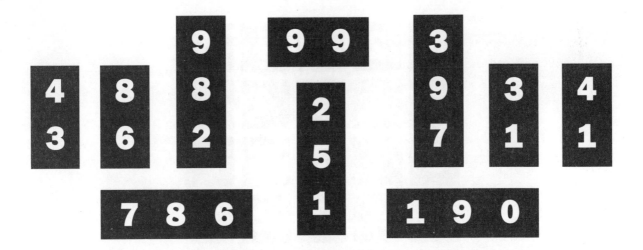

NUMBER PUZZLE 66

Place the tiles in a square to give some five-figure numbers. When
this has been done accurately the same
five numbers can be read both downwards and across.
How does the finished square look?

ANSWER 34

NUMBER PUZZLE 67

Start in the middle circle and move from circle to touching circle.
Collect the four numbers which will total 15. Once a route has
been found return to the middle circle and start again.
If a route can be found, which obeys the above rules but follows
both a clockwise and an anticlockwise path, it is treated as two
different routes. How many different ways are there?

ANSWER 76

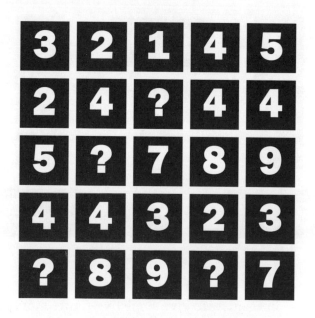

NUMBER PUZZLE 68

Which number should replace the question marks in the diagram?

ANSWER 24

NUMBER PUZZLE 69

You have three shots with each go to score 26. Aim at this target and work out how many different ways there are to make the score. Assume each shot scores and once three numbers have been used the same three cannot be used again in another order.
How many are there?

ANSWER 66

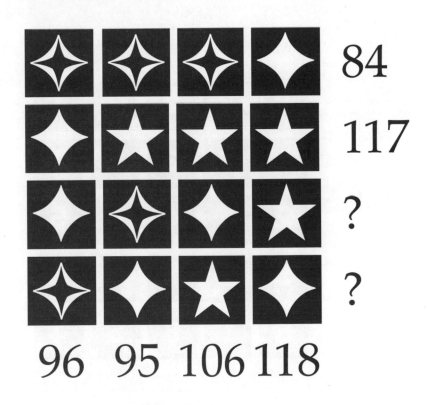

84

117

?

?

96 95 106 118

NUMBER PUZZLE 70

The contents of each box has a value. The total of the values is shown alongside a row or beneath a column. Which number should replace the question marks?

ANSWER 14

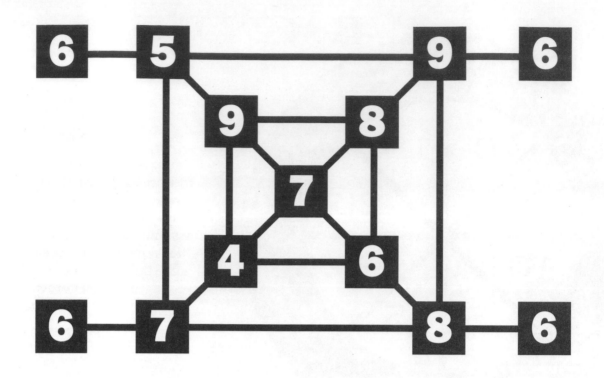

NUMBER PUZZLE 71

Start at any corner number and collect another four numbers by
following the paths shown. Add the five numbers together.
What is the highest number you can score?

ANSWER 55

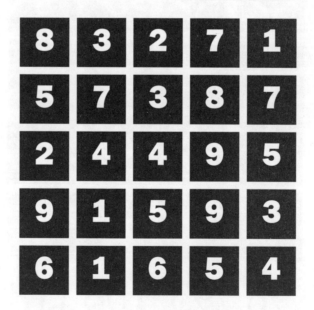

NUMBER PUZZLE 72

Move from square to adjacent square either vertically or horizontally. Begin at the bottom left-hand square and end at the top right-
hand square. Collect nine numbers and total them.
What is the lowest possible score?

ANSWER 3

A B C D E

A	B	C	D	E
9	2	9	7	
5	2	5	3	1
5	1	6	4	3
5	0	7	5	
6	3	5	3	0

NUMBER PUZZLE 73

There is a relationship between the columns of numbers in this diagram. The letters above the grid are there to help you. Which number should be placed in the empty squares?

ANSWER 96

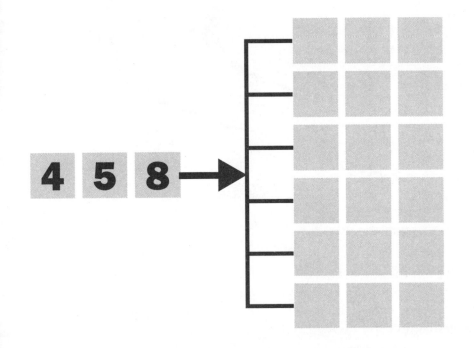

NUMBER PUZZLE 74

Place six three digit numbers of 100 plus at the end of 458 so that six numbers of six digits are produced. When each number is divided by 122 six whole numbers can be found. Which numbers should be placed in the grid?

ANSWER 44

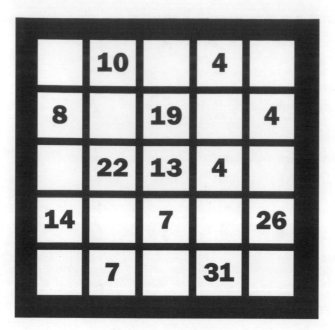

NUMBER PUZZLE 75

Each row, column and five-figure diagonal line
in this diagram must total 65. Two different numbers must be
used, as many times as necessary, to achieve this.
What are the numbers?

ANSWER 85

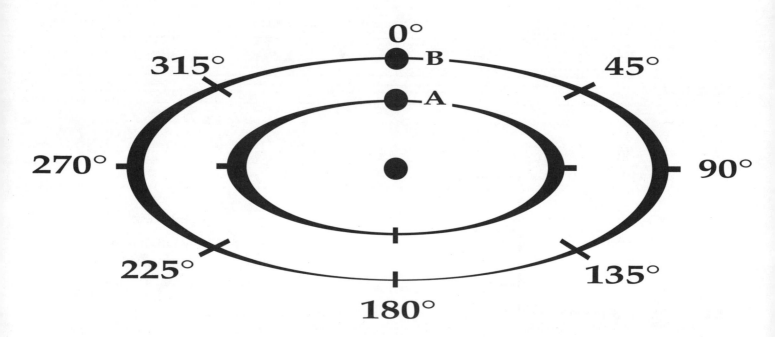

NUMBER PUZZLE 76

Two planets are in line with each other and the sun.
The outer planet will orbit the sun every fifteen years. The inner
planet takes five years. Both move in a clockwise direction. When
will they next form a straight line with each other and the sun?
The diagram should help you.

ANSWER 33

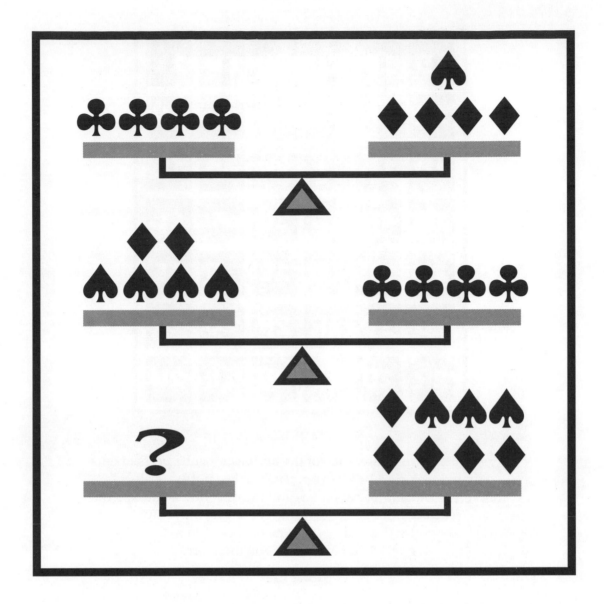

NUMBER PUZZLE 77

The top two scales are in perfect balance.
How many clubs will be needed to balance the bottom set?

ANSWER 75

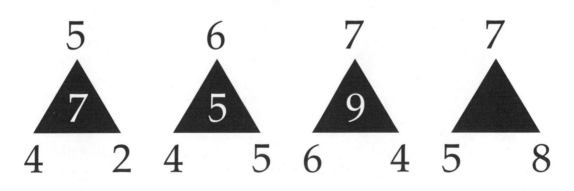

NUMBER PUZZLE 78

Which figure should be placed in the empty triangle?

ANSWER 23

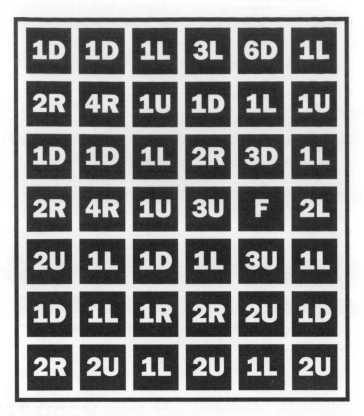

NUMBER PUZZLE 79

Here is an unusual safe. Each of the buttons must be pressed once
only in the correct order to open it. The last button is always
marked F. The number of moves and the direction is marked on
each button. Thus 1U would mean one move up
whilst 1L would mean one move to the left.
Which button is the first you must press.

ANSWER 65

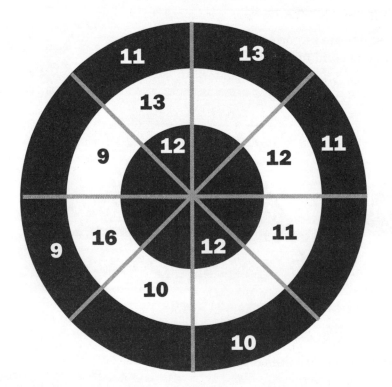

NUMBER PUZZLE 80

Complete the grid in such a way
that each segment of three numbers
totals the same.
When this has been done correctly
each of the three concentric circles of
eight numbers will produce
identical totals.
Now complete the diagram.

ANSWER 13

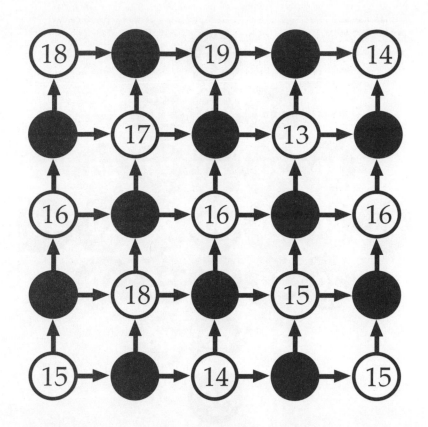

NUMBER PUZZLE 81

Move from the bottom left-hand corner to the top right-hand
corner following the arrows. Add the numbers on your route
together. If each black spot is worth minus 7,
how many different routes are there to score 51?

ANSWER 54

NUMBER PUZZLE 82

Place the tiles in the square to give some five-figure numbers.
When this has been done accurately the same
five numbers can be read both down and across.
How does the finished square look?

ANSWER 2

NUMBER PUZZLE 83

Start in the middle circle and move from circle to touching circle.
Collect the four numbers which will total 100. Once a route has
been found return to the middle circle and start again.
If a route can be found, which obeys the above rules but follows
both a clockwise and an anticlockwise path, it is treated as two
different routes.
How many different ways are there?

ANSWER 95

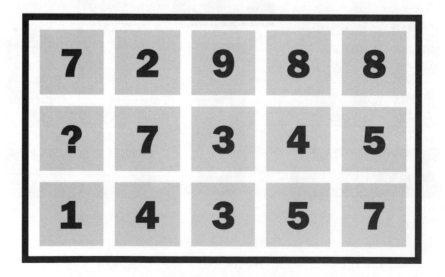

NUMBER PUZZLE 84

Which number should replace the question mark in the diagram?

ANSWER 43

NUMBER PUZZLE 85

You have three shots with each go to score 42. Aim at this target and work out how many different ways there are to make the score. Assume each shot scores and once three numbers have been used the same three cannot be used again in another order.
How many are there?

ANSWER 84

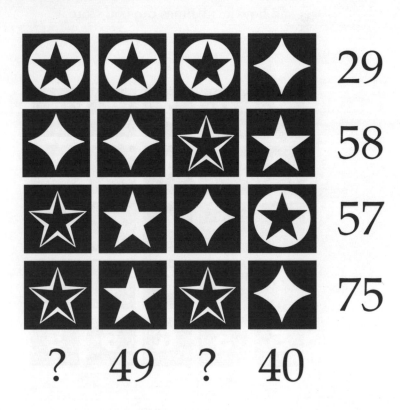

29

58

57

75

? 49 ? 40

NUMBER PUZZLE 86

The contents of each box has a value. The total of the values is shown alongside a row or beneath a column. Which number should replace the question mark?

ANSWER 32

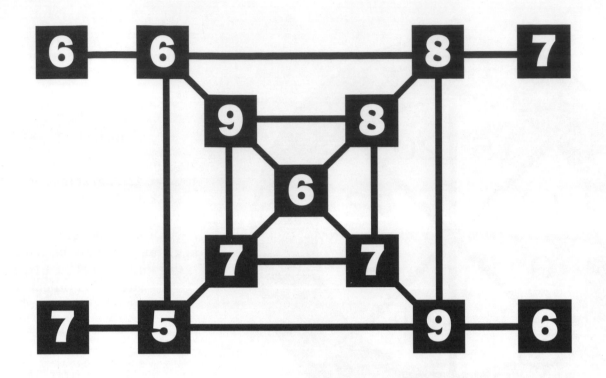

NUMBER PUZZLE 87

Start at any corner number and collect another four numbers by
following the paths shown. Add the five numbers together.
What is the highest number you can score
and how many times can you score it?

ANSWER 74

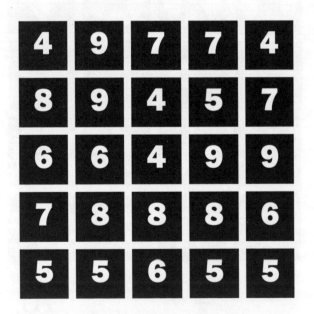

NUMBER PUZZLE 88

Move from square to adjacent square either vertically or horizontally. Begin at the bottom left-hand square and end at the top right-
hand square. Collect nine numbers and total them.
How many times can you score 60?

ANSWER 22

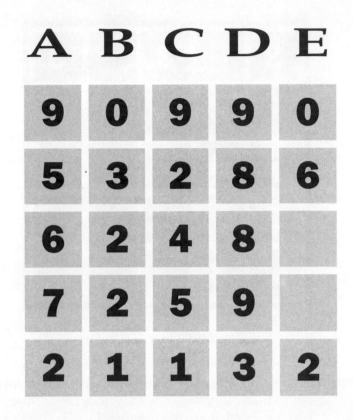

A B C D E

A	B	C	D	E
9	0	9	9	0
5	3	2	8	6
6	2	4	8	
7	2	5	9	
2	1	1	3	2

NUMBER PUZZLE 89

There is a relationship between the columns of numbers in this diagram. The letters above the grid are there to help you. Which number should be placed in the empty squares?

ANSWER 64

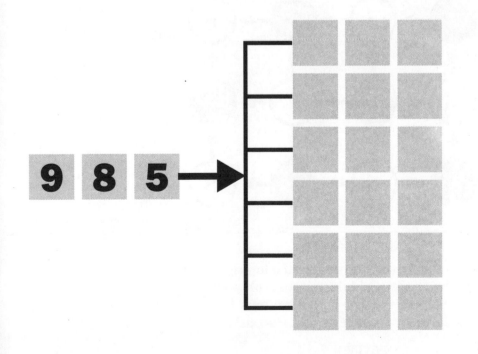

NUMBER PUZZLE 90

Place six three digit numbers of 100 plus at the end of 985 so that six numbers of six digits are produced. When each number is divided by 133 six whole numbers can be found. Which numbers should be placed in the grid?

ANSWER 12

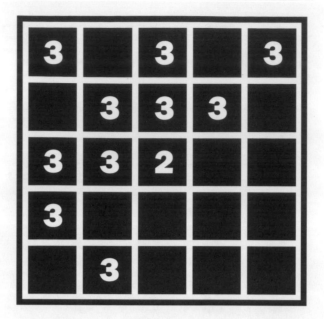

NUMBER PUZZLE 91

Each row, column and five-figure diagonal line
in this diagram must total 10. Three different numbers must be
used, as many times as necessary, to achieve this.
What are the numbers?

ANSWER 53

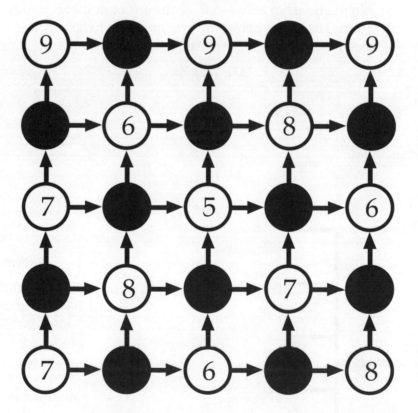

NUMBER PUZZLE 92

Move from the bottom left-hand corner to the top right-hand
corner following the arrows. Add the numbers on your route
together. If each black spot is worth minus 4,
what is the lowest number you can score?

ANSWER 1

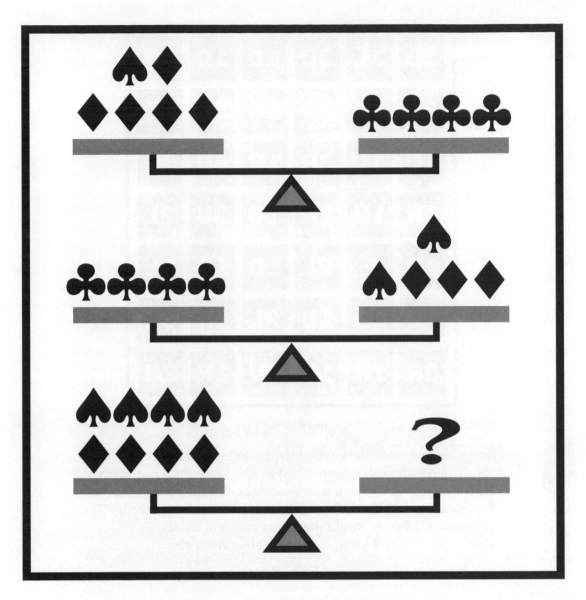

NUMBER PUZZLE 93

The top two scales are in perfect balance.
How many clubs will be needed to balance the bottom set?

ANSWER 42

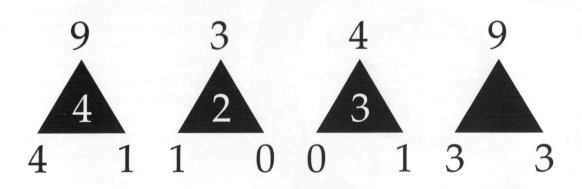

NUMBER PUZZLE 94

Which figure should be placed in the empty triangle?

ANSWER 94

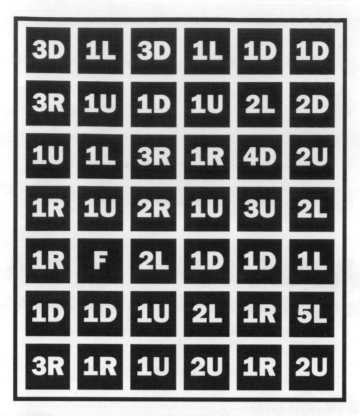

NUMBER PUZZLE 95

Here is an unusual safe. Each of the buttons must be pressed once only in the correct order to open it. The last button is always marked F. The number of moves and the direction is marked on each button. Thus 1U would mean one move upwards whilst 1L would mean one move to the left.
Which button is the first you must press.

ANSWER 83

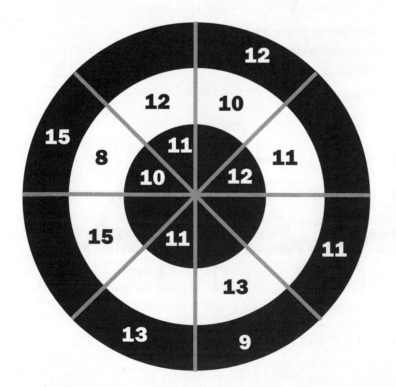

NUMBER PUZZLE 96

Complete the grid in such a way that each segment of three numbers totals the same.
When this has been done correctly each of the three concentric circles of eight numbers will produce three identical totals.
Now complete the diagram.

ANSWER 31

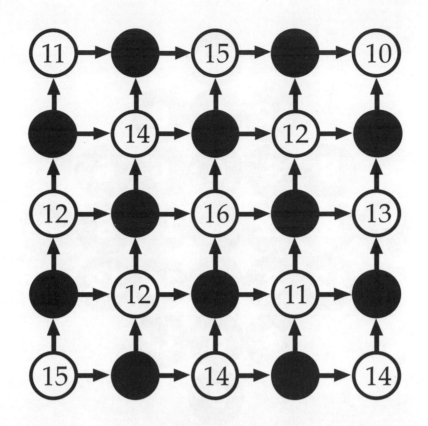

NUMBER PUZZLE 97

Move from the bottom left-hand corner to the top right-hand
corner following the arrows. Add the numbers on your route
together. If each black spot is worth minus 3,
which number can be scored only once?

ANSWER 73

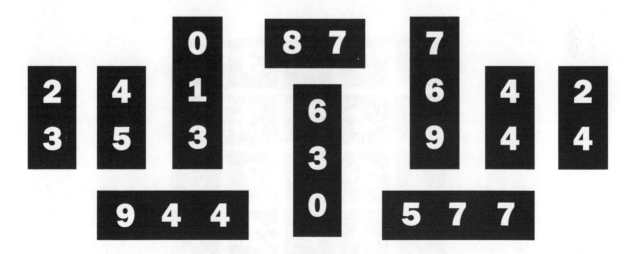

NUMBER PUZZLE 98

Place the tiles in a square to give some five-figure numbers. When
this has been done accurately the same
five numbers can be read both down and across.
How does the finished square look?

ANSWER 21

NUMBER PUZZLE 99

Start in the middle circle and move from circle to touching circle.
Collect the four numbers which will total 30. Once a route has
been found return to the middle circle and start again.
If a route can be found, which obeys the above rules but follows
both a clockwise and an anticlockwise path, it is treated as two
different routes. How many different ways are there?

ANSWER 63

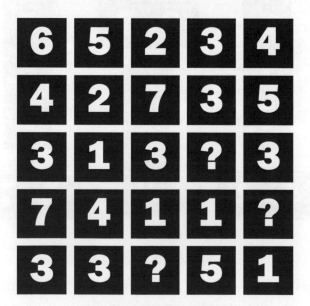

NUMBER PUZZLE 100

Which number should replace the question marks in the diagram?

ANSWER 11

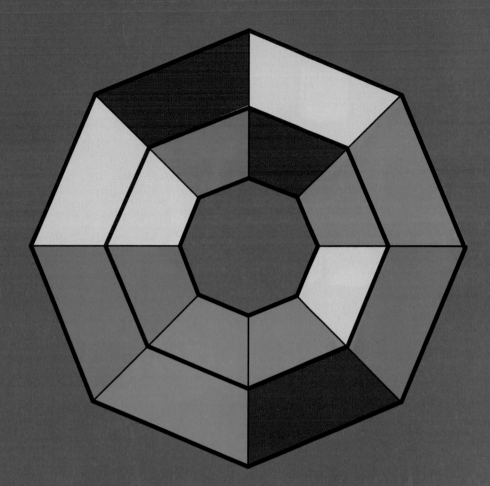

BLUE NUMBER PUZZLE 1

A segment in the diagram is divided into two parts.
Each like part has the same value. When the four
values of two opposing segments are added together
they can be divided by the value of one of the parts.
Which part is this?

ANSWER 1 ON LAST PAGE OF THIS SECTION

BLUE NUMBER PUZZLE 2

Each like box in the diagram has the
same value. The boxes are arranged in
three series. The first series gives a total
of 35, the second series 63 and the third
series 27. It is easy to discover the value
of the red box, if you look carefully.
What are the values of the yellow and
blue boxes?

ANSWER 4 ON LAST PAGE OF THIS
SECTION

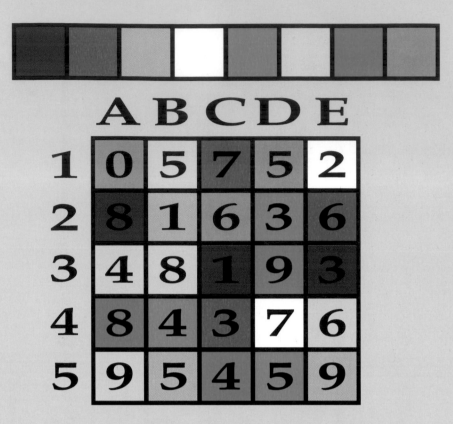

YELLOW NUMBER PUZZLE 1

Select a tile from the grid that matches one in the number frame.
Place it in the frame and choose the next tile. When eight tiles have
been placed correctly a number divisible by 9,876 will appear.
Divide the number to get a year. Marry the year to June 18th
and discover an historical event.
What was the year and what was the event?

ANSWER 1 ON LAST PAGE OF THIS SECTION

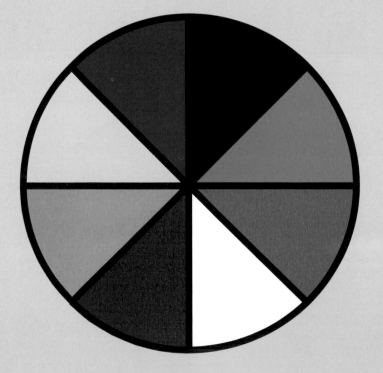

YELLOW NUMBER PUZZLE 2

In the diagram each segment has a value.
The red, green, and purple segments are
worth 3 each. The blue and the yellow segments are worth 6. The remaining
segments are worth 0. Three segments
must be added together to give a total of 9.
A segment can be used twice but once a
combination has been used it cannot
be reused in another order.
How many different
combinations are there?

ANSWER 6 ON LAST PAGE
OF THIS SECTION

RED NUMBER PUZZLE 1

Here are four distinctly, different boxes. A number of these
boxes have been arranged in the grid. Each like
box has the same value. The total of the values is shown
alongside a row or beneath a column.
Which number should replace the question marks?

ANSWER 1 ON LAST PAGE OF THIS SECTION

RED NUMBER PUZZLE 2

When the correct eight segments are rearranged to form a circle
the sum of four of the segments will equal the sum of the other
four. Yellow segments represent either 2, 4, 9, or 11. Blue segments
represent either 1, 3, 5, or 7. White segments represent either 6, 8,
10, or 12. Green segments represent either 13, 14, 19, or 20.
What are the totals and the sequence of segments?

ANSWER 5 ON LAST PAGE OF THIS SECTION

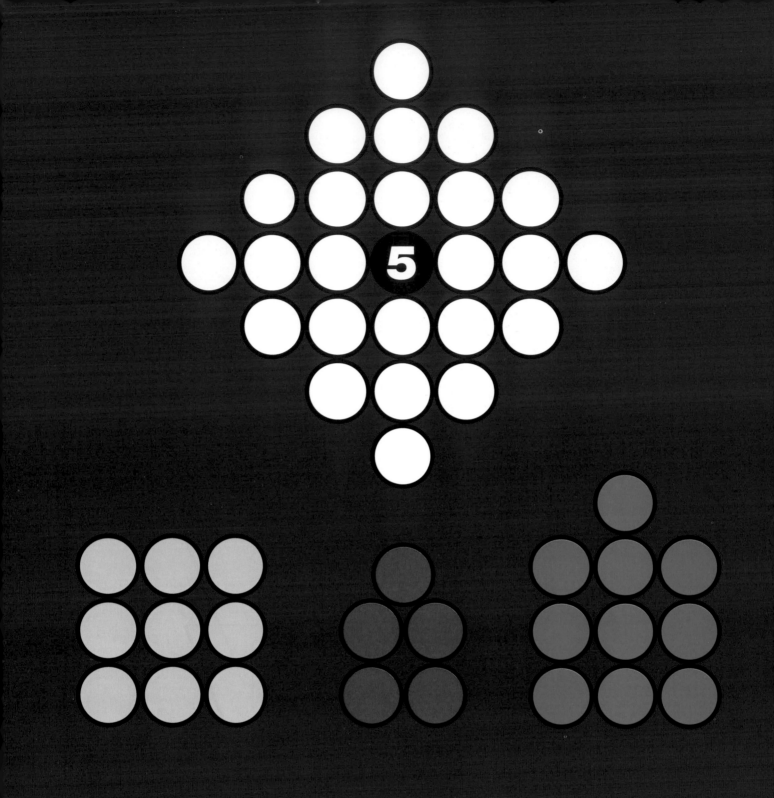

RED NUMBER PUZZLE 3

Fill the diagram up with the circles. The black circle goes
in the middle and is worth 5. Yellow circles are 10s,
red circles are 30s, and green circles are 35s.
When the correct pattern has been found, by moving
from circle to touching circle, in each case starting from the black
circle, a total of 80 can be reached 12 times.
What does the pattern look like?

ANSWER 2 ON LAST PAGE OF THIS SECTION

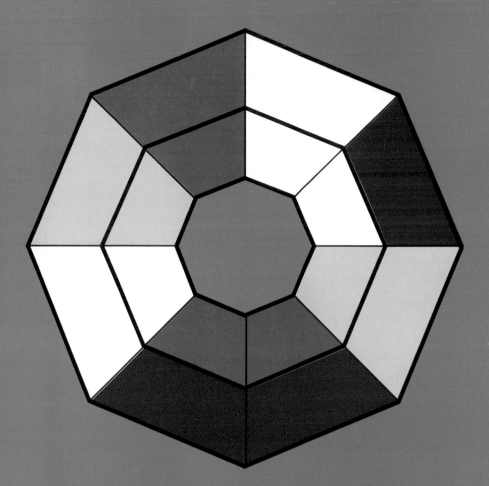

GREEN NUMBER PUZZLE 1

A segment in the diagram is divided into two parts.
Each like part has the same value. When the four
values of two opposing segments are added together
they can be divided by the value of one of the parts in the
diagram. Which part is this?

ANSWER 1 ON LAST PAGE OF THIS SECTION

GREEN NUMBER PUZZLE 2

Each like box in the diagram has the
same value. The boxes are arranged in
three series. The first series gives a total
of 25, the second series 53 and the third
series 63. It is easy to discover the value
of the red box, if you look carefully.
What are the values of the yellow and
blue boxes?

ANSWER 4 ON LAST PAGE OF THIS
SECTION

A B C D E

	A	B	C	D	E
1	0	8	9	3	9
2	2	6	4	7	5
3	7	3	8	0	9
4	5	1	3	5	4
5	2	9	2	4	1

BLUE NUMBER PUZZLE 3

Select a tile from the grid that matches on in the number frame.
Place it in the frame and choose the next tile. When eight tiles have
been placed correctly a number divisible by 34,567 will appear.
Divide the number to get a year. Marry the year to November 22nd
and discover an historical event.
What was the year and what was the event?

ANSWER 2 ON LAST PAGE OF THIS SECTION

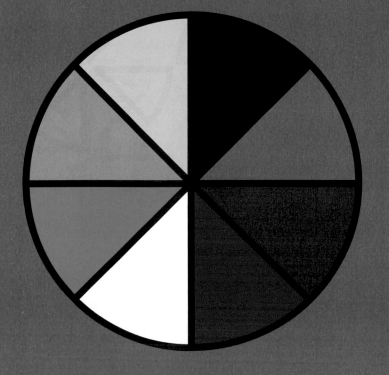

BLUE NUMBER PUZZLE 4

In the diagram each segment has a value.
The black, orange, white and green
segments are worth 5 each. The blue and
the purple segments are worth 2. The
remaining segments are worth 0. Three
segments must be added together to give
a total of 7. A segment can be used twice
but once a combination has been used
it cannot be reused in another order.
How many different
combinations are there?

ANSWER 5 ON LAST PAGE OF THIS
SECTION

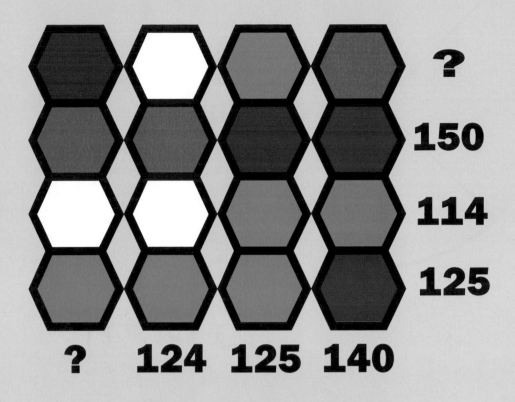

?

150

114

125

? 124 125 140

YELLOW NUMBER PUZZLE 3

Here are four distinctly, different boxes. A number of these
boxes have been arranged in the grid. Each like
box has the same value. The total of the values is shown
alongside a row or beneath a column.
Which number should replace the question marks?

ANSWER 2 ON LAST PAGE OF TIIIS SECTION

YELLOW NUMBER PUZZLE 4

When the correct eight segments are rearranged to form circle the
sum of four of the segments will equal the sum of the other four.
White segments represent either 1, 4, 9, or 15. Blue segments
represent either 6, 8, 10, or 17. Red segments represent either 3, 5,
11, or 12. Green segments represent either 2, 13, 14, or 16.
What are the totals and the sequence of segments?

ANSWER 7 ON LAST PAGE OF THIS SECTION

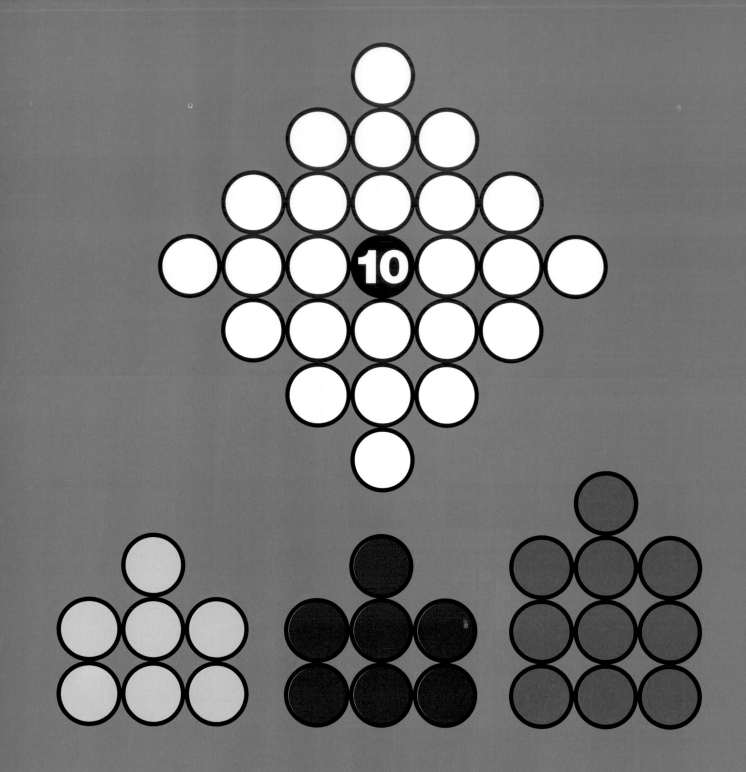

GREEN NUMBER PUZZLE 3

Fill the diagram up with the circles. The black circle goes
in the middle and is worth 10. Yellow circles are 15s,
blue circles are 40s, and red circles are 25s.
When the correct pattern has been found, by moving
from circle to touching circle,.in each case starting from the black
circle, a total of 90 can be reached 9 times.
What does the pattern look like?

ANSWER 2 ON LAST PAGE OF THIS SECTION

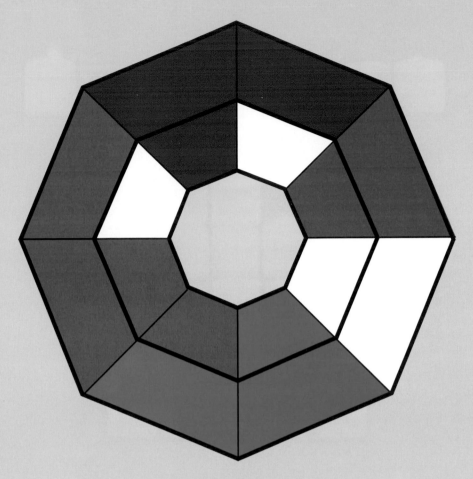

YELLOW NUMBER PUZZLE 5

A segment in the diagram is divided into two parts.
Each like part has the same value. When the four
values of two opposing segments are added together
they can be divided by the value of one of the parts of the
diagram. Which part is this?

ANSWER 3 ON LAST PAGE OF THIS SECTION

YELLOW NUMBER PUZZLE 6

Each like box in the diagram has the
same value. The boxes are arranged in
three series. The first series gives a total
of 43, the second series 35 and the third
series 32. The red box is worth 5.
What are the values of the white, green
and blue boxes?

ANSWER 8 ON LAST PAGE OF THIS
SECTION

A B C D E

	A	B	C	D	E
1	7	3	7	8	0
2	0	9	8	1	9
3	1	3	6	6	5
4	2	4	5	2	4
5	9	8	1	7	9

YELLOW NUMBER PUZZLE 7

Select a tile from the grid that matches on in the number frame.
Place it in the frame and choose the next tile. When eight tiles have
been placed correctly a number divisible by 5,605 will appear.
Divide the number to get a year. Marry the year to July 21st
and discover an historical event.
What was the year and what was the event?

ANSWER 4 ON LAST PAGE OF THIS SECTION

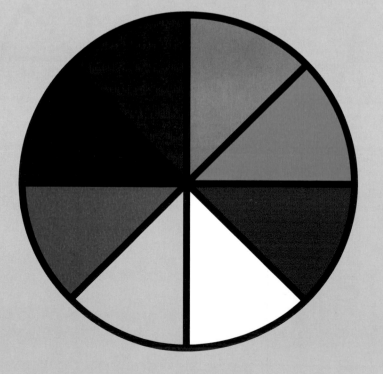

YELLOW NUMBER PUZZLE 8

In the diagram each segment has a value.
The red, purple, and blue segments are
worth 2 each. The orange and the white
segments are worth 0. The remaining
segments are worth 4. Three segments
must be added together to give a total of 8.
A segment can be used twice but once a
combination has been used it cannot
be reused in another order.
How many different
combinations are there?

ANSWER 9 ON LAST PAGE OF
THIS SECTION

RED NUMBER PUZZLE 4

Here are four distinctly, different boxes. A number of these boxes have been arranged in the grid. Each like box has the same value. The total of the values is shown alongside a row or beneath a column.
Which number should replace the question marks?

ANSWER 3 ON LAST PAGE OF THIS SECTION

RED NUMBER PUZZLE 5

When the correct eight segments are rearranged to form a circle the sum of four of the segments will equal the sum of the other four. Yellow segments represent either 4, 5, 6, or 7. Blue segments represent either 1, 8, 10, or 15. White segments represent either 2, 9, 14, or 17. Green segments represent either 3, 11, 13, or 16. What are the totals and the sequence of segments?

ANSWER 6 ON LAST PAGE OF THIS SECTION

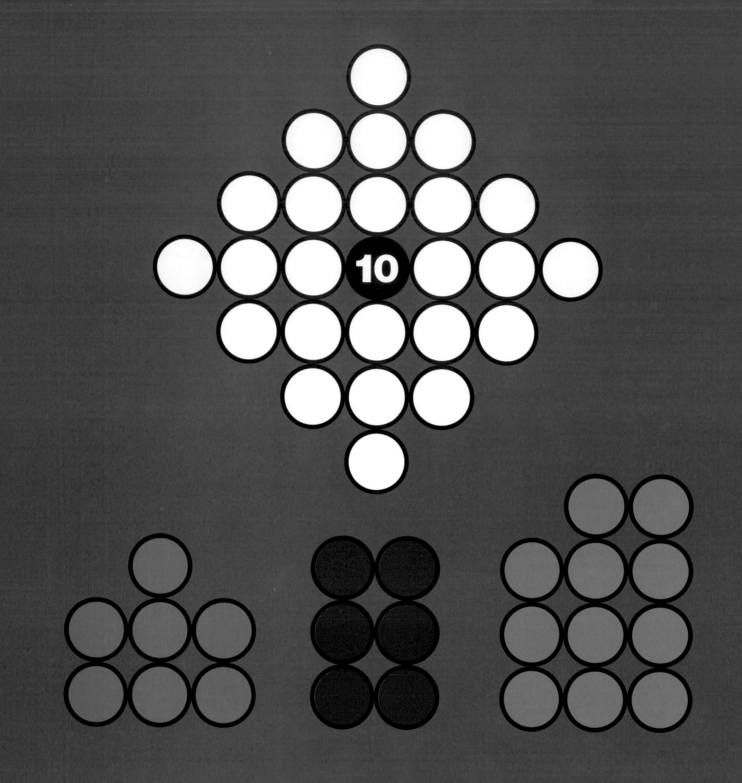

BLUE NUMBER PUZZLE 5

Fill the diagram up with the circles. The black circle goes
in the middle and is worth 5. Green circles are 30s,
red circles are 10s, and blue circles are 15s.
When the correct pattern has been found, by moving from circle to
touching circle, in each case starting from the black circle, a total of
60 can be reached 8 times. What does the pattern look like?

ANSWER 3 ON LAST PAGE OF THIS SECTION

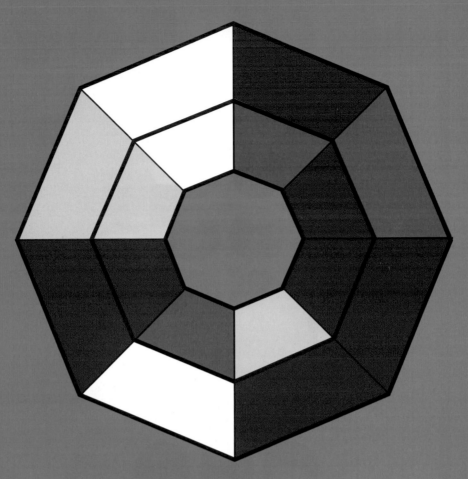

GREEN NUMBER PUZZLE 4

A segment in the diagram is divided into two parts.
Each like part has the same value. When the four
values of two opposing segments are added together
they can be divided by the value of one of the parts in the
diagram. Which part is this?

ANSWER 3 ON LAST PAGE OF THIS SECTION

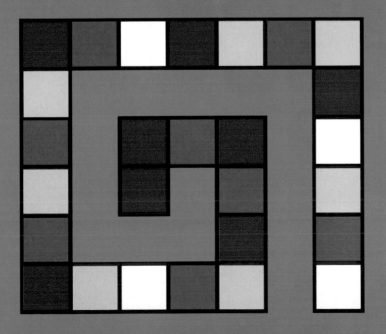

GREEN NUMBER PUZZLE 5

Each like box in the diagram has the
same value. The boxes are arranged in
three series. The first series gives a total
of 49, the second series 35 and the third
series 42. The red box is worth 3.
What are the values of the white,
yellow and blue boxes?

ANSWER 5 ON LAST PAGE OF THIS
SECTION

A B C D E

	A	B	C	D	E
1	7	6	5	2	3
2	1	9	4	9	4
3	2	4	1	7	6
4	7	6	8	3	0
5	0		8	4	8

RED NUMBER PUZZLE 6

Select a tile from the grid that matches on in the number frame.
Place it in the frame and choose the next tile. When eight tiles have
been placed correctly a number divisible by 8,888 will appear.
Divide the number to get a year. Marry the year to July 14th
and discover an historical event.
What was the year and what was the event?

ANSWER 4 ON LAST PAGE OF THIS SECTION

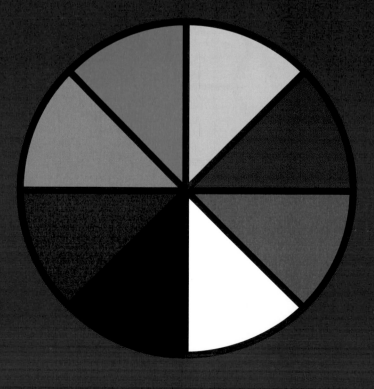

RED NUMBER PUZZLE 7

In the diagram each segment has a value.
The green, yellow, purple, black and blue
are worth 0 each. The remaining segments
are worth 5. Three segments must be
added together to give a total of 5.
A segment can be used twice but once a
combination has been used it cannot be
reused in another order.
How many different
combinations are there?

ANSWER 7 ON LAST PAGE OF THIS
SECTION

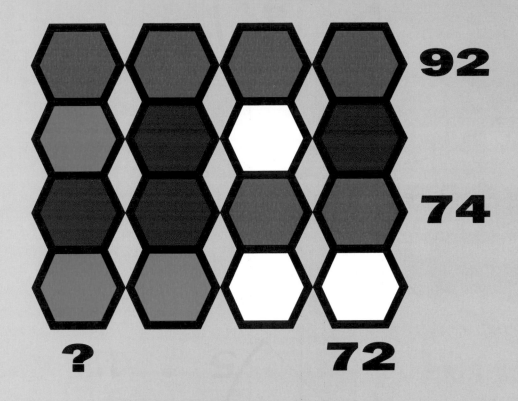

YELLOW NUMBER PUZZLE 9

Here are four distinctly, different boxes. A number of these
boxes have been arranged in the grid. Each like
box has the same value. The total of the values is shown
alongside a row or beneath a column.
Which number should replace the question marks?

ANSWER 5 ON LAST PAGE OF THIS SECTION

YELLOW NUMBER PUZZLE 10

When the correct eight segments are rearranged to form a circle
the sum of four of the segments will equal the sum of the other
four. White segments represent either 1, 4, 15, or 16. Blue segments
represent either 6, 9, 11, or 12. Red segments represent either 3, 4, 7,
or 8. Green segments represent either 2, 5, 10, or 13.
What are the totals and the sequence of segments?

ANSWER 10 ON LAST PAGE OF THIS SECTION

Blue Number Puzzles

1.   The red part. A yellow part is worth 8, a blue part 3, a green part 4 and a red part 7.

2.   1963. The assassination of President Kennedy. The number is 67855021.

3.

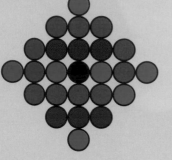

4.   Blue is worth 5 Yellow 8.

5.   16.

Yellow Number Puzzles

1.   1815. The Battle of Waterloo. The number is 17924940.

2.   132.

3.   The white part. A white part is worth 4, a green 13, a blue 8 and a red 3.

4.   1969. The first moon walk. The number is 11036245.

5.   59.

6.   28.

7.   12. Four red segments equal two white plus two green segments. The sequence reads red, red, white, green, red, red, white, and green.

8.   A blue box is worth 6, a green is worth 4 and a white is worth 2.

9.   30.

10.   30. Four green segments equal two red plus two blue. The sequence reads red, blue, green,green, red, blue, green, green.

Red Number Puzzles

1.   72.

2.

3.   53.

4.   1789. The storming of the Bastille. The number is 15900632.

5.   18. Yellow , blue, white, blue, yellow, blue, white, blue. Yellow, yellow, blue and blue total 18, as do white, white, blue and blue.

6.   22. Four yellow segments equal two blue plus two green segments. The sequence reads blue, green, yellow, yellow, blue, green, yellow, yellow.

7.   45.

Green Number Puzzles

1.   The yellow part. A white part is worth 5, a yellow 7, a blue 12 and a red 13.

2.

3.   The white part. A yellow part is worth 9, a white 5, a blue 2 and a red 6.

4.   Blue is worth 1 and orange 5.

5.   Yellow is worth 6, blue 4, and white 7.

NUMBER PUZZLE 101

You have four shots with each go to score 62. Aim at this target and work out how many different ways there are to make the score. Assume each shot scores and once four numbers have been used the same four cannot be used again in another order.
How many are there?

ANSWER 52

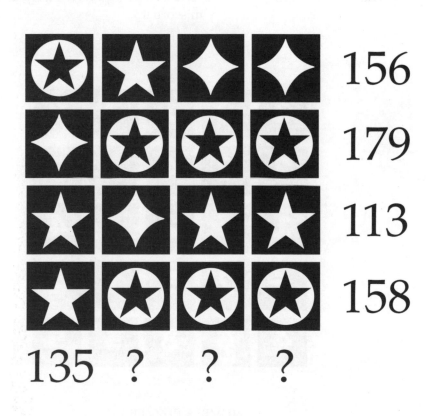

NUMBER PUZZLE 102

The contents of each box has a value. The total of the values is shown alongside a row or beneath a column. Which number should replace the question mark?

ANSWER 104

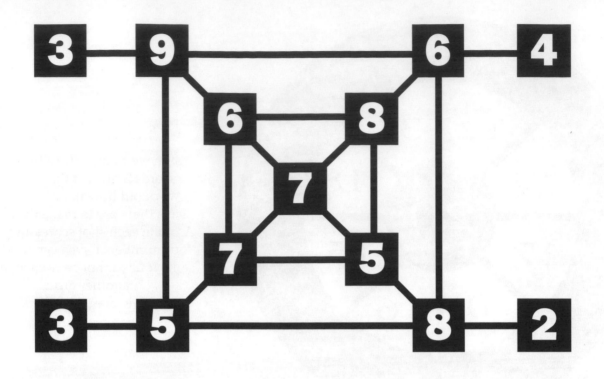

NUMBER PUZZLE 103

Start at the corner number and collect another four numbers by
following the paths shown. Add the five numbers together.
What is the lowest number you can score and how many times can
you score it?

ANSWER 93

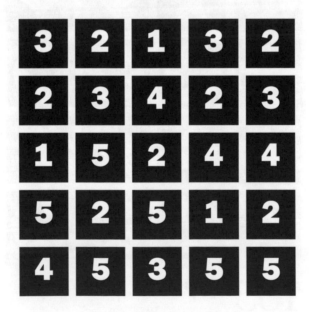

NUMBER PUZZLE 104

Move from square to adjacent square either vertically or
horizontally. Begin at the bottom left-hand square and end at the
top right-hand square. Collect nine numbers and total them.
How many different ways are there to total 31?

ANSWER 41

A B C D E

A	B	C	D	E
6	3	5	8	8
7	3	6	9	9
5	3	4	7	7
6	0	2	5	2
5	0	1	4	

NUMBER PUZZLE 105

There is a relationship between the columns of numbers in this diagram. The letters above the grid are there to help you. Which number should be placed in the empty squares?

ANSWER 167

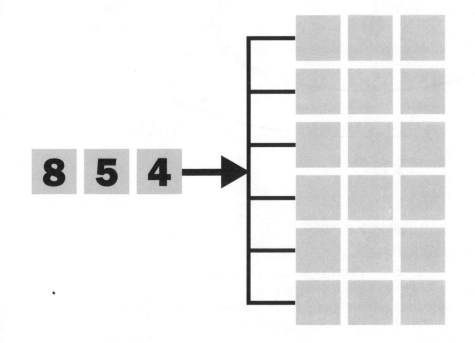

NUMBER PUZZLE 106

Place six three digit numbers of 100 plus at the end of 854 so that six numbers of six digits are produced. When each number is divided by 149 six whole numbers can be found. Which numbers should be placed in the grid?

ANSWER 115

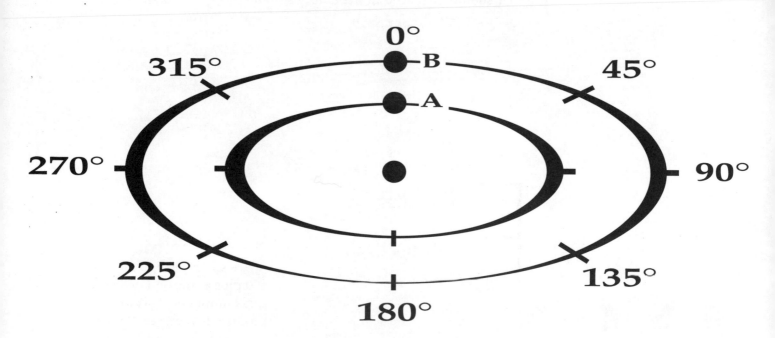

	2		1	
2				1
			2	2
	2	2	2	6
2		2		2

NUMBER PUZZLE 107

Each row, column and five-figure diagonal line
in this diagram must total 15. Three different numbers must be
used, as many times as necessary, to achieve this.
What are the numbers?

ANSWER 187

NUMBER PUZZLE 108

Two planets are in line with each other and the sun.
The outer planet will orbit the sun every one hundred years. The
inner planet takes twenty years. Both move in a clockwise
direction. When will they next form a straight line with each other
and the sun? The diagram should help you.

ANSWER 156

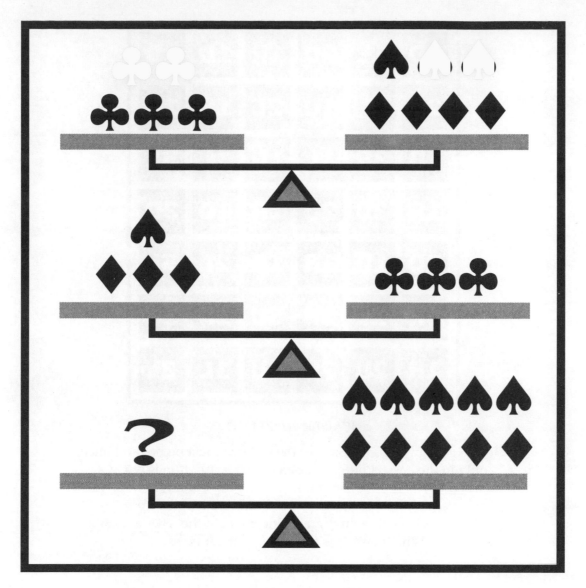

NUMBER PUZZLE 109

The top two scales are in perfect balance.
How many clubs will be needed to balance the bottom set?

ANSWER 197

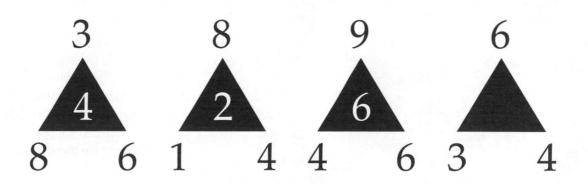

NUMBER PUZZLE 110

Which number should be placed in the empty triangle?

ANSWER 145

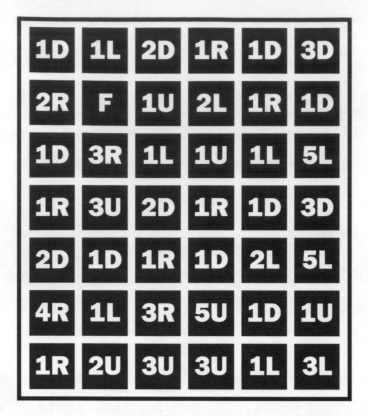

1D	1L	2D	1R	1D	3D
2R	F	1U	2L	1R	1D
1D	3R	1L	1U	1L	5L
1R	3U	2D	1R	1D	3D
2D	1D	1R	1D	2L	5L
4R	1L	3R	5U	1D	1U
1R	2U	3U	3U	1L	3L

NUMBER PUZZLE 111

Here is an unusual safe. Each of the buttons must be pressed once
only in the correct order to open it. The last button is always
marked F. The number of moves and the direction is marked on
each button. Thus 1U would mean one move up
whilst 1L would mean one move to the left.
Which button is the first you must press?

ANSWER 166

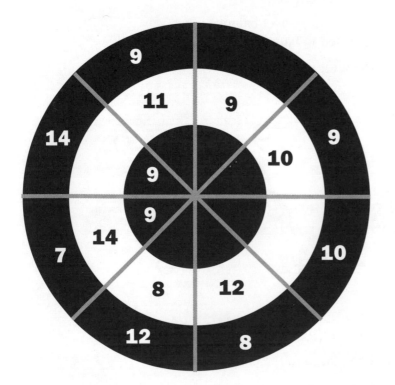

NUMBER PUZZLE 112

Complete the grid in such a way
that each segment of three numbers
totals the same.
When this has been done correctly
each of the three concentric circles of
eight numbers will produce
identical totals.
Now complete the diagram.

ANSWER 114

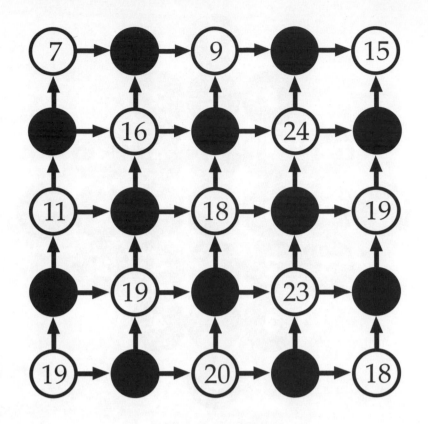

NUMBER PUZZLE 113

Move from the bottom left-hand corner to the top right-hand
corner following the arrows. Add the numbers on your route
together. If each black spot is worth minus 17,
how many different routes are there to score 2?

ANSWER 135

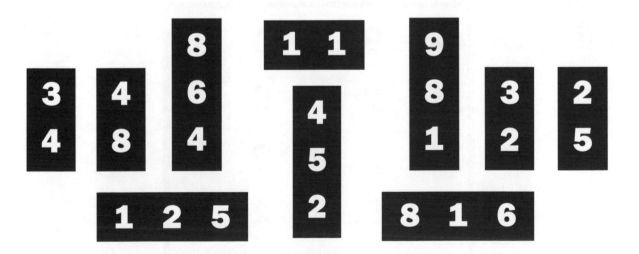

NUMBER PUZZLE 114

Place the tiles in a square to give some five-figure numbers.
When this has been done accurately the same
five numbers can be read both down and across.
How does the finished square look?

ANSWER 155

NUMBER PUZZLE 115

Start in the middle circle and move from circle to touching circle.
Collect the four numbers which will total 10. Once a route has
been found return to the middle circle and start again.
If a route can be found, which obeys the above rules but follows
both a clockwise and an anticlockwise path, it is treated as two
different routes. How many different ways are there?

ANSWER 196

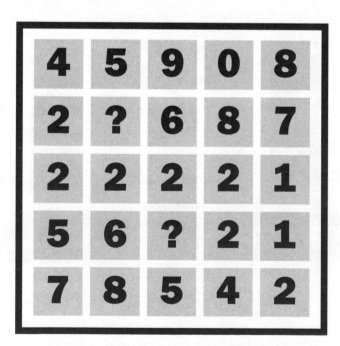

NUMBER PUZZLE 116

Which number should replace the question marks in the diagram?

ANSWER 144

NUMBER PUZZLE 117

You have five shots with each go to score 22. Aim at this target and work out how many different ways there are to make the score. Assume each shot scores and once five numbers have been used the same five cannot be used again in another order.
How many are there?

ANSWER 186

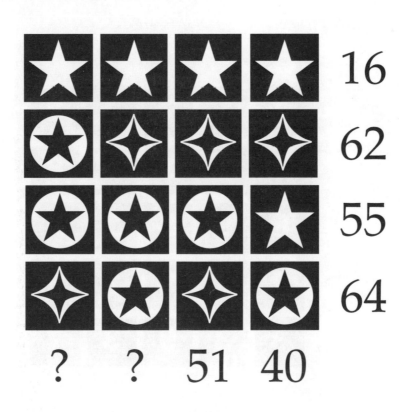

NUMBER PUZZLE 118

The contents of each box has a value. The total of the values is shown alongside a row or beneath a column. Which number should replace the question marks?

ANSWER 134

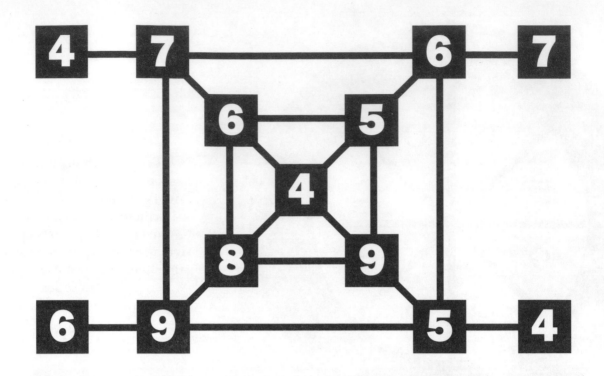

NUMBER PUZZLE 119

Start at any corner number and collect another four numbers by following the paths shown. Add the five numbers together. How many times can you score 37?

ANSWER 176

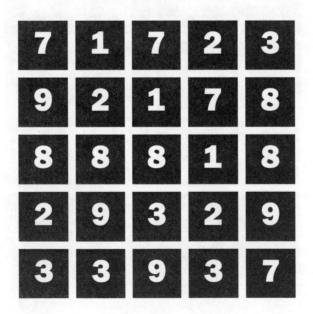

NUMBER PUZZLE 120

Move from square to adjacent square either vertically or horizontally. Begin at the bottom left-hand square and end at the top right-hand square. Collect nine numbers and total them. How many different ways are there to total 46?

ANSWER 124

A B C D E

A	B	C	D	E
7	5	2	3	7
9	4	5	6	9
8	7	1	2	
8	4	4	5	
5	3	2	3	5

NUMBER PUZZLE 121

There is a relationship between the columns of numbers in this diagram. The letters above the grid are there to help you. Which number should be placed in the empty squares?

ANSWER 165

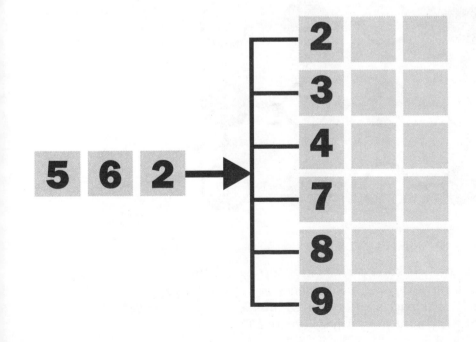

NUMBER PUZZLE 122

Place six three digit numbers of 100 plus at the end of 562 so that six numbers of six digits are produced. When each number is divided by 61.5 six whole numbers can be found. In this case, the first numbers are given. Which numbers should be placed inthe grid?

ANSWER 113

NUMBER PUZZLE 123

Each row, column and five-figure diagonal line
in this diagram must total 20. Three different numbers must be
used, as many times as necessary, to achieve this.
What are the numbers?

ANSWER 125

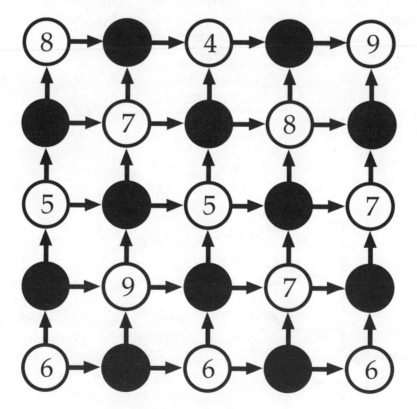

NUMBER PUZZLE 124

Move from the bottom left-hand corner to the top right-hand
corner following the arrows. Add the numbers on your route
together. If each black spot is worth minus 3,
how many different ways can you score 20?

ANSWER 154

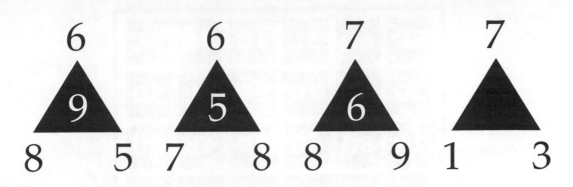

NUMBER PUZZLE 125

Which figure should be placed in the empty triangle?

ANSWER 143

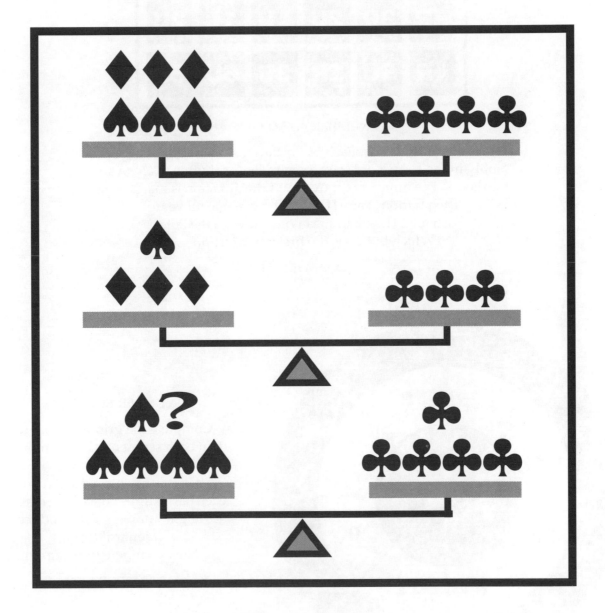

NUMBER PUZZLE 126

The top two scales are in perfect balance.
How many diamonds will be needed to balance the bottom set?

ANSWER 195

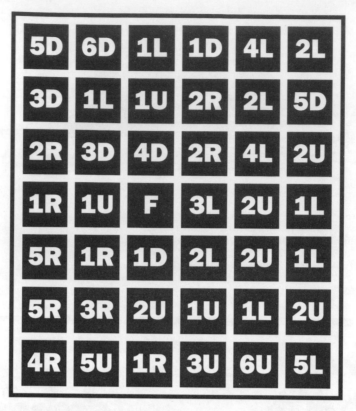

5D	6D	1L	1D	4L	2L
3D	1L	1U	2R	2L	5D
2R	3D	4D	2R	4L	2U
1R	1U	F	3L	2U	1L
5R	1R	1D	2L	2U	1L
5R	3R	2U	1U	1L	2U
4R	5U	1R	3U	6U	5L

NUMBER PUZZLE 127

Here is an unusual safe. Each of the buttons must be pressed once
only in the correct order to open it. The last button is always
marked F. The number of moves and the direction is marked on
each button. Thus 1U would mean one move up
whilst 1L would mean one move to the left.
Which button is the first you must press?

ANSWER 185

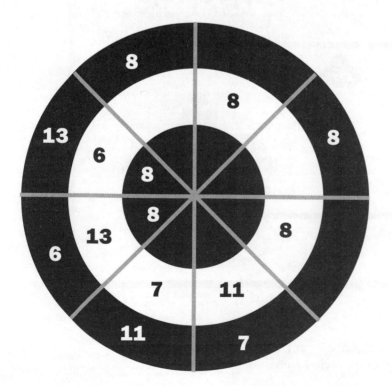

NUMBER PUZZLE 128

Complete the grid in such a way
that each segment of three numbers
totals the same.
When this has been done correctly
each of the three concentric circles of
eight numbers will produce
identical totals.
Now complete the diagram.

ANSWER 133

NUMBER PUZZLE 129

Start in the middle circle and move from circle to touching circle.
Collect the four numbers which will total 53. Once a route has
been found return to the middle circle and start again.
If a route can be found, which obeys the above rules but follows
both a clockwise and an anticlockwise path, it is treated as two
different routes. How many different ways are there?

ANSWER 175

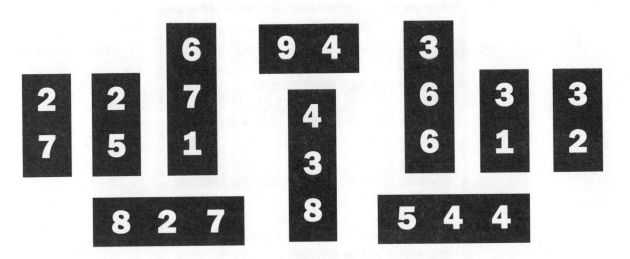

NUMBER PUZZLE 130

Place the tiles in a square to give some five-figure numbers. When
this has been done accurately the same
five numbers can be read both down and across.
How does the finished square look?

ANSWER 123

NUMBER PUZZLE 131

Start in the middle circle and move from circle to touching circle.
Collect the four numbers which will total 49. Once a route has
been found return to the middle circle and start again.
If a route can be found, which obeys the above rules but follows
both a clockwise and an anticlockwise path, it is treated as two
different routes. How many different ways are there?

ANSWER 164

NUMBER PUZZLE 132

Which number should replace the question marks in the diagram?

ANSWER 112

NUMBER PUZZLE 133

You have five shots with each go to score 61. Aim at this target and work out how many different ways there are to make the score. Assume each shot scores and once five numbers have been used the same five cannot be used again in another order.
How many ways are there?

ANSWER 177

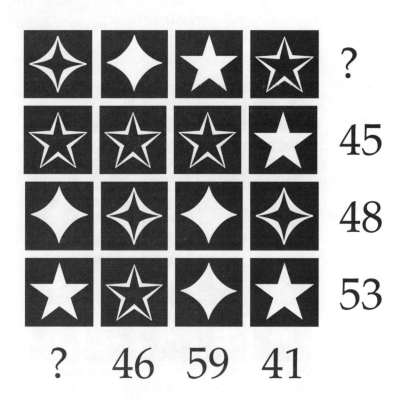

NUMBER PUZZLE 134

The contents of each box has a value. The total of the values is shown alongside a row or beneath a column. Which number should replace the question marks?

ANSWER 153

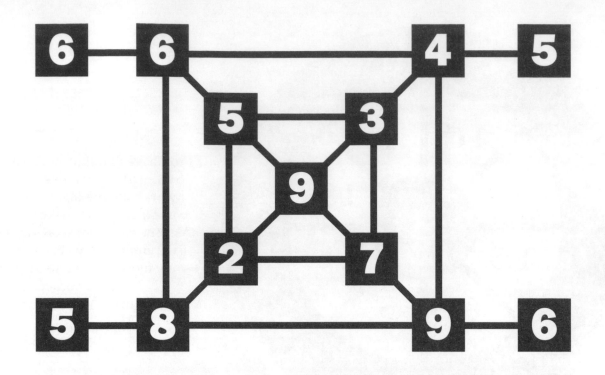

NUMBER PUZZLE 135

Start at any corner number and collect another four numbers by
following the paths shown. Add the five numbers together.
How many times can you score 38?

ANSWER 194

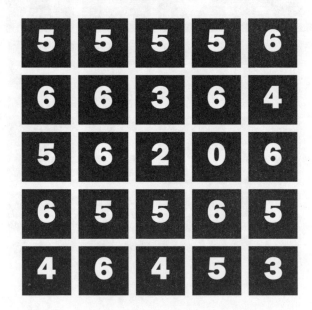

NUMBER PUZZLE 136

Move from square to adjacent square either vertically or
horizontally. Begin at the bottom left-hand square and end at the
top right-hand square. Collect nine numbers and total them.
How many different ways are there to total 48?

ANSWER 142

A B C D E

A	B	C	D	E
6	2	6	4	
4	1	5	3	
6	1	7	5	4
3	1	4	2	1
8	4	6	4	0

NUMBER PUZZLE 137

There is a relationship between the columns of numbers in this diagram. The letters above the grid are there to help you. Which number should be placed in the empty squares?

ANSWER 184

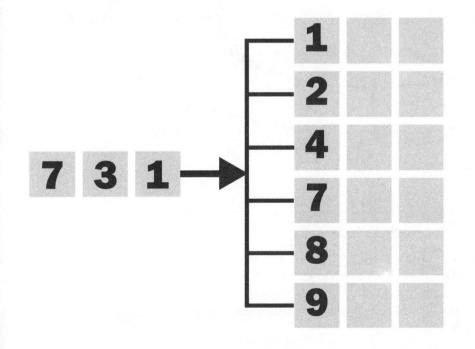

NUMBER PUZZLE 138

Place six three digit numbers of 100 plus at the end of 731 so that six numbers of six digits are produced. When each number is divided by 39.5 six whole numbers can be found. In this case, the first numbers are given. Which numbers should be placed inthe grid?

ANSWER 132

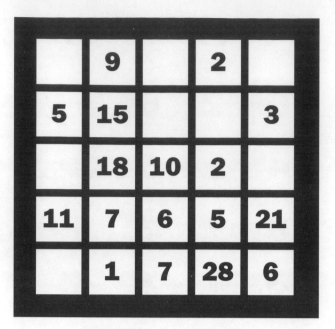

NUMBER PUZZLE 139

Each row, column and five-figure diagonal line
in this diagram must total 50. Four different numbers must be
used, as many times as necessary, to achieve this.
What are the numbers?

ANSWER 174

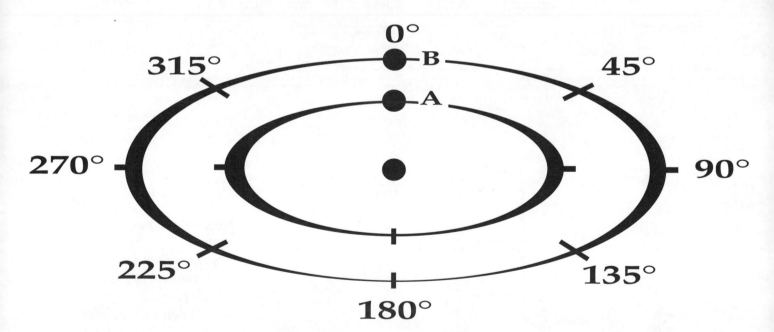

NUMBER PUZZLE 140

Two planets are in line with each other and the sun.
The outer planet will orbit the sun every 36 years. The inner
planet takes 4 years. Both move in a clockwise direction. When
will they next form a straight line with each other and the sun?
The diagram should help you.

ANSWER 122

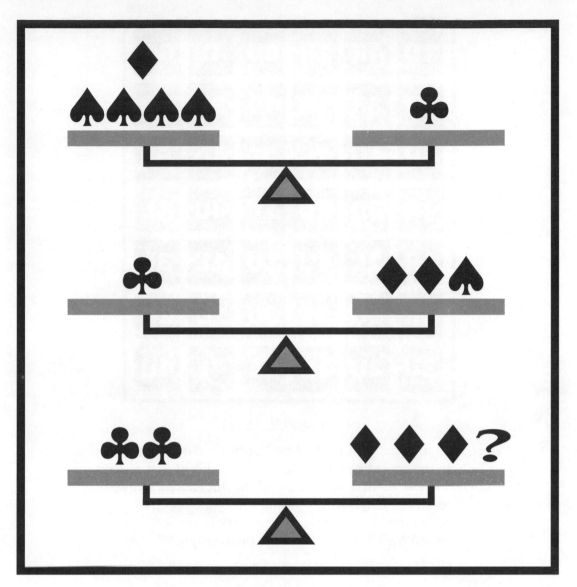

NUMBER PUZZLE 141

The top two scales are in perfect balance.
How many spades will be needed to balance the bottom set?

ANSWER 163

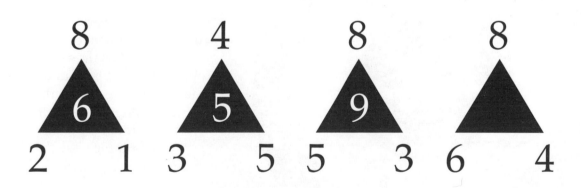

NUMBER PUZZLE 142

Which figure should be placed in the empty triangle?

ANSWER 111

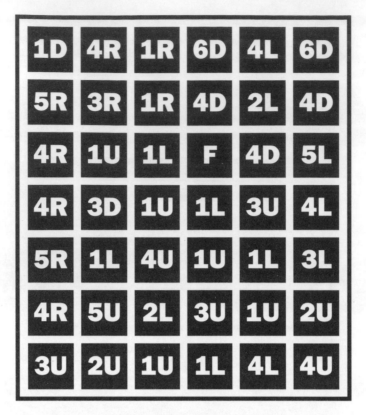

NUMBER PUZZLE 143

Here is an unusual safe. Each of the buttons must be pressed once
only in the correct order to open it. The last button is always
marked F. The number of moves and the direction is marked on
each button. Thus 1U would mean one move up
whilst 1L would mean one move to the left.
Which button is the first you must press?

ANSWER 146

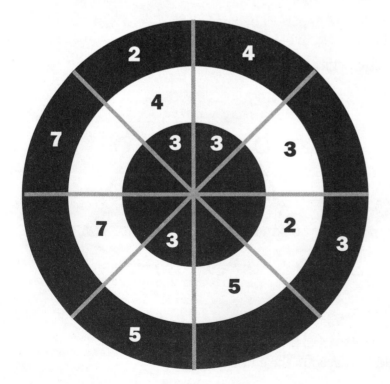

NUMBER PUZZLE 144

Complete the grid in such a way
that each segment of three numbers
totals the same.
When this has been done correctly
each of the three concentric circles of
eight numbers will produce
identical totals.
Now complete the diagram.

ANSWER 152

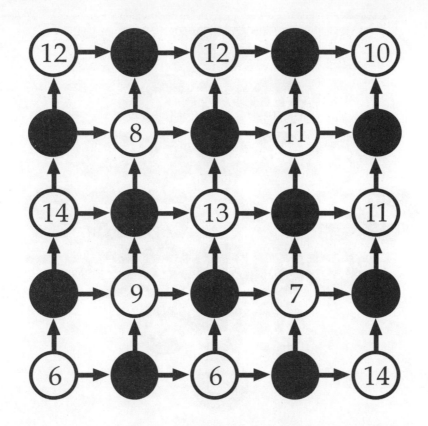

NUMBER PUZZLE 145

Move from the bottom left-hand corner to the top right-hand
corner following the arrows. Add the numbers on your route
together. If each black spot is worth minus 7,
how many different times can you score 22?

ANSWER 193

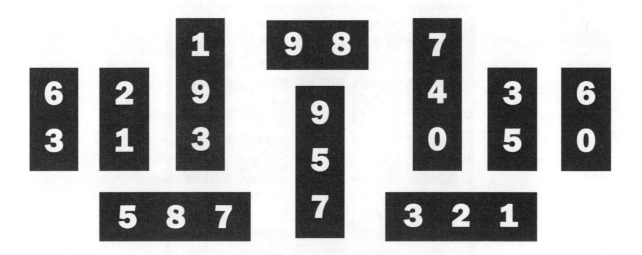

NUMBER PUZZLE 146

Place the tiles in a square to give some five-figure numbers.
When this has been done accurately the same
five numbers can be read both down and across.
How does the finished square look?

ANSWER 141

NUMBER PUZZLE 147

Start in the middle circle and move from circle to touching circle.
Collect the four numbers which will total 45. Once a route has
been found return to the middle circle and start again.
If a route can be found, which obeys the above rules but follows
both a clockwise and an anticlockwise path, it is treated as two
different routes. How many different ways are there?

ANSWER 183

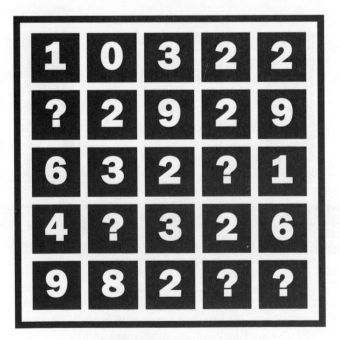

NUMBER PUZZLE 148

Which number should replace the question marks in the diagram?

ANSWER 131

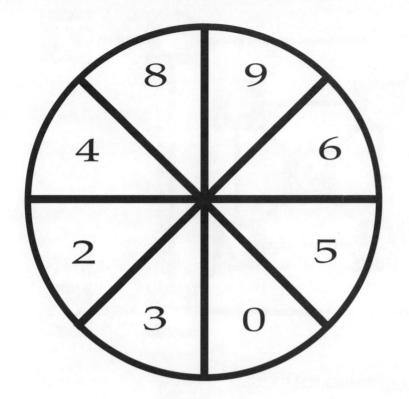

NUMBER PUZZLE 149

You have three shots with each go to score 18. Aim at this target and work out how many different ways there are to make the score. Assume each shot scores and once three numbers have been used the same three cannot be used again in another order.
How many are there?

ANSWER 173

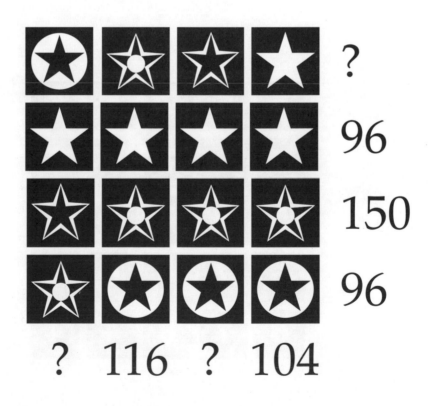

NUMBER PUZZLE 150

The contents of each box has a value. The total of the values is shown alongside a row or beneath a column. Which number should replace the question marks?

ANSWER 121

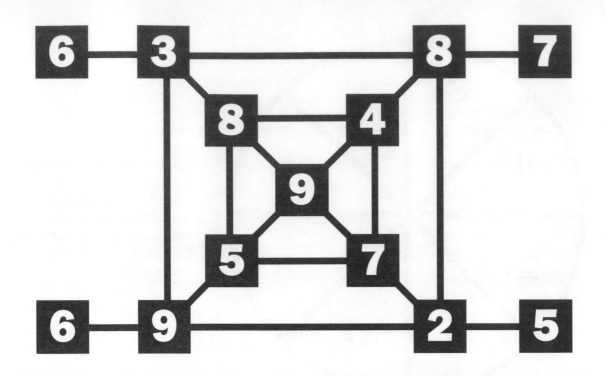

NUMBER PUZZLE 151

Start at any corner number and collect another four numbers by
following the paths shown. Add the five numbers together.
How many ways can you score 36?

ANSWER 162

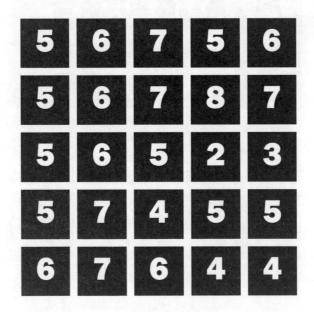

NUMBER PUZZLE 152

Move from square to adjacent square either vertically or
horizontally. Begin at the bottom left-hand square and end at the
top right-hand square. Collect nine numbers and total them.
What is the highest score possible?

ANSWER 110

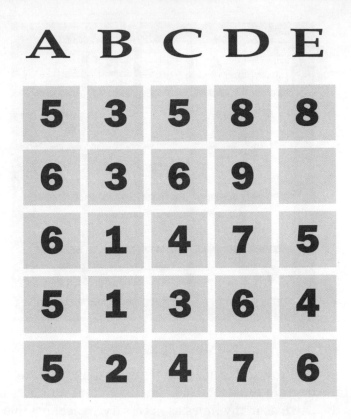

NUMBER PUZZLE 153

There is a relationship between the columns of numbers in this diagram. The letters above the grid are there to help you. Which number should be placed in the empty square?

ANSWER 198

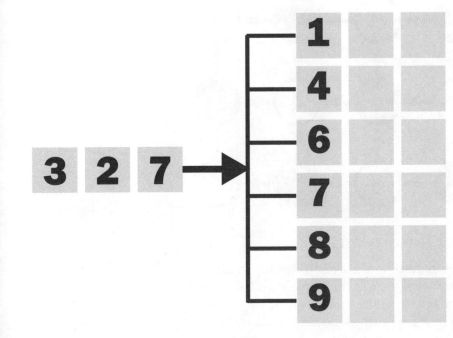

NUMBER PUZZLE 154

Place six three digit numbers of 100 plus at the end of 327 so that six numbers of six digits are produced. When each number is divided by 27.5 six whole numbers can be found. In this case, the first numbers are given. Which numbers should be placed inthe grid?

ANSWER 151

	4		5	
4				5
		12	7	7
	7	7	7	
7		7		7

NUMBER PUZZLE 155

Each row, column and five-figure diagonal line
in this diagram must total 60. Three different numbers must
be used, as many times as necessary, to achieve this.
What are the numbers?

ANSWER 192

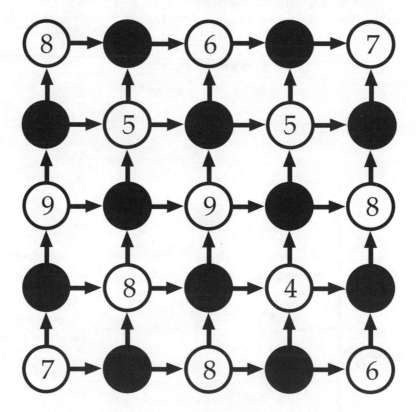

NUMBER PUZZLE 156

Move from the bottom left-hand corner to the top right-hand
corner following the arrows. Add the numbers on your route
together. If each black spot is worth 13,
which two numbers can be scored once only?

ANSWER 140

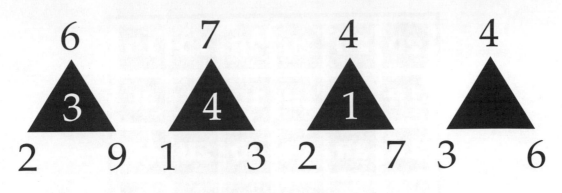

NUMBER PUZZLE 157

Which figure should be placed in the empty triangle?

ANSWER 130

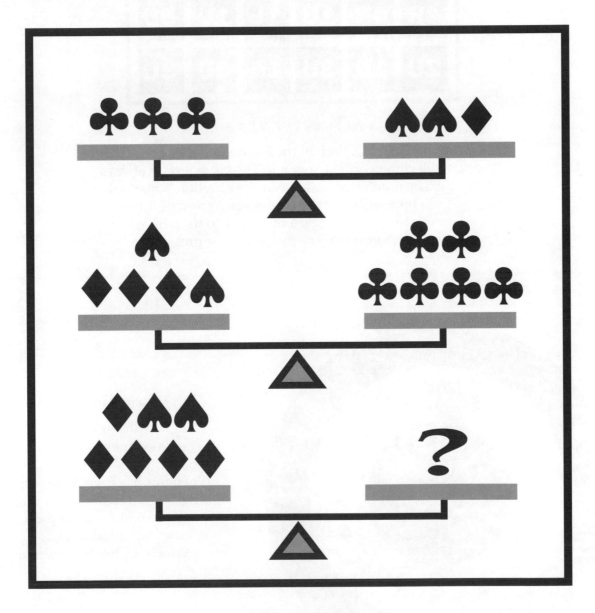

NUMBER PUZZLE 158

The top two scales are in perfect balance.
How many clubs will be needed to balance the bottom set?

ANSWER 182

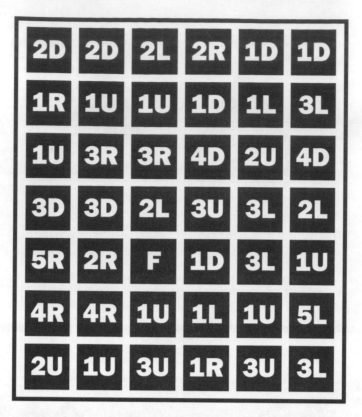

2D	2D	2L	2R	1D	1D
1R	1U	1U	1D	1L	3L
1U	3R	3R	4D	2U	4D
3D	3D	2L	3U	3L	2L
5R	2R	F	1D	3L	1U
4R	4R	1U	1L	1U	5L
2U	1U	3U	1R	3U	3L

NUMBER PUZZLE 159

Here is an unusual safe. Each of the buttons must be pressed once only in the correct order to open it. The last button is always marked F. The number of moves and the direction is marked on each button. Thus 1U would mean one move up whilst 1L would mean one move to the left.
Which button is the first you must press?

ANSWER 172

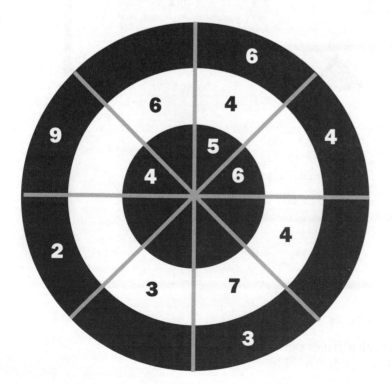

NUMBER PUZZLE 160

Complete the grid in such a way that each segment of three numbers totals the same.
When this has been done correctly each of the three concentric circles of eight numbers will produce identical totals.
Now complete the diagram.

ANSWER 120

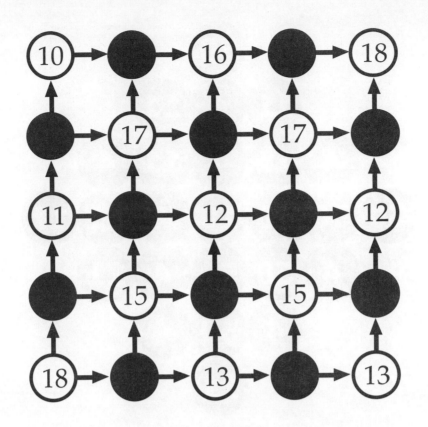

NUMBER PUZZLE 161

Move from the bottom left-hand corner to the top right-hand
corner following the arrows. Add the numbers on your route
together. If each black spot is worth minus 9,
how many times can you score 41?

ANSWER 161

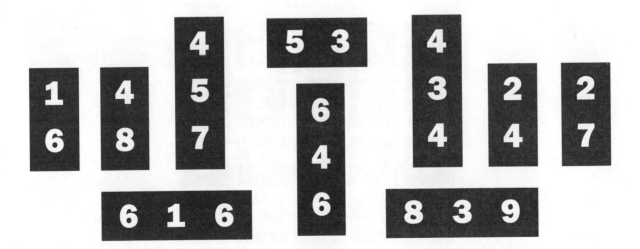

NUMBER PUZZLE 162

Place the tiles in a square to give some five-figure numbers. When
this has been done accurately the same
five numbers can be read both down and across.
How does the finished square look?

ANSWER 109

NUMBER PUZZLE 163

Start in the middle circle and move from circle to touching circle.
Collect the four numbers which will total 75. Once a route has
been found return to the middle circle and start again.
If a route can be found, which obeys the above rules but follows
both a clockwise and an anticlockwise path, it is treated as two
different routes. How many different ways are there?

ANSWER 202

NUMBER PUZZLE 164

Which number should replace the question marks in the diagram?

ANSWER 150

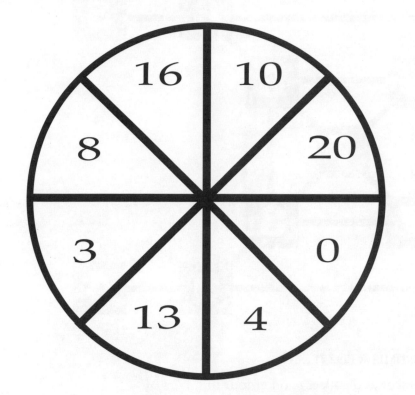

NUMBER PUZZLE 165

You have five shots with each go to score 56. Aim at this target and work out how many different ways there are to make the score. Assume each shot scores and once five numbers have been used the same five cannot be used again in another order.
How many ways are there?

ANSWER 191

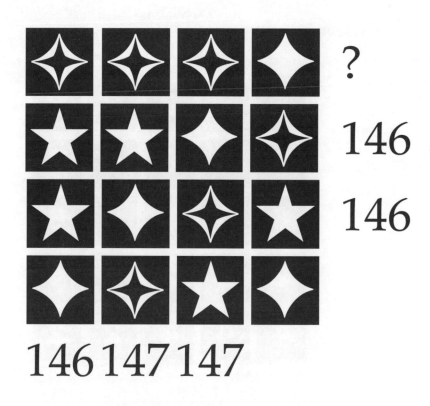

NUMBER PUZZLE 166

The contents of each box has a value. The total of the values is shown alongside a row or beneath a column. Which number should replace the question mark?

ANSWER 139

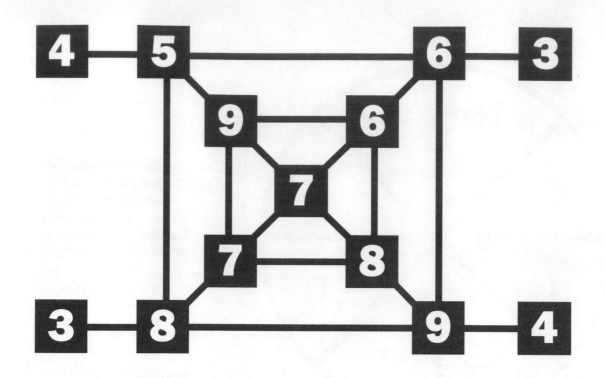

NUMBER PUZZLE 167

Start at any corner number and collect another four numbers by
following the paths shown. Add the five numbers together.
How many times can you score less than 30?

ANSWER 181

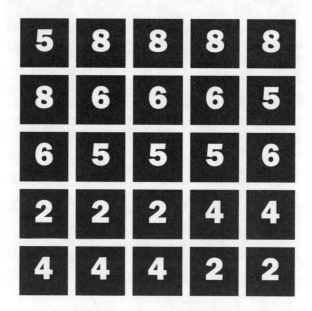

NUMBER PUZZLE 168

Move from square to adjacent square either vertically or horizontally. Begin at the bottom left-hand square and end at the top
right-hand square. Collect nine numbers and total them.
What are the highest and lowest numbers you can score?

ANSWER 129

A B C D E

A	B	C	D	E
6	2	5	8	
3	2	2	5	4
2	1	0	3	1
4	3	4	7	
4	2	3	6	5

NUMBER PUZZLE 169

There is a relationship between the columns of numbers in this diagram. The letters above the grid are there to help you. Which number should be placed in the empty squares?

ANSWER 171

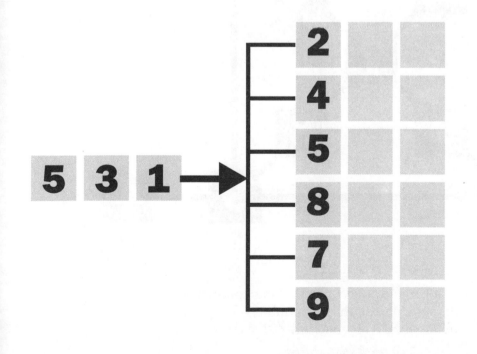

NUMBER PUZZLE 170

Place six three digit numbers of 100 plus at the end of 531 so that six numbers of six digits are produced. When each number is divided by 40.5 six whole numbers can be found. In this case, the first numbers are given. Which numbers should be placed inthe grid?

ANSWER 119

	10	16	1	13
9		14		2
14		11		
				25
9	8	6	25	

NUMBER PUZZLE 171

Each row, column and five-figure diagonal line
in this diagram must total 55. Three different numbers must be
used, as many times as necessary, to achieve this.
What are these numbers?

ANSWER 160

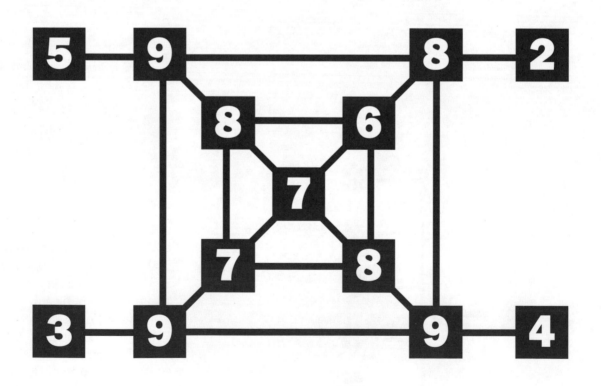

NUMBER PUZZLE 172

Start at any corner number and collect another four numbers by
following the paths shown. Add the five numbers together.
How many times can you score 40?

ANSWER 108

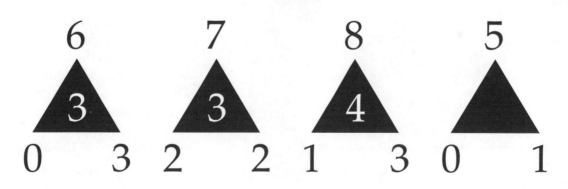

NUMBER PUZZLE 173

The top two scales are in perfect balance.
How many spades will be needed to balance the bottom set?

ANSWER 201

NUMBER PUZZLE 174

Which figure should be placed in the empty triangle?

ANSWER 149

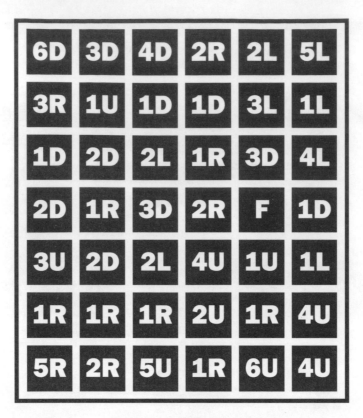

NUMBER PUZZLE 175

Here is an unusual safe. Each of the buttons must be pressed once
only in the correct order to open it. The last button is always
marked F. The number of moves and the direction is marked on
each button. Thus 1U would mean one move up
whilst 1L would mean one move to the left.
Which button is the first you must press?

ANSWER 190

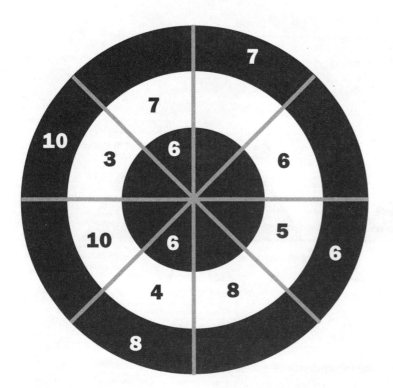

NUMBER PUZZLE 176

Complete the grid in such a way
that each segment of three numbers
totals the same.
When this has been done correctly
each of the three concentric circles of
eight numbers will produce
identical totals.
Now complete the diagram.

ANSWER 13 8

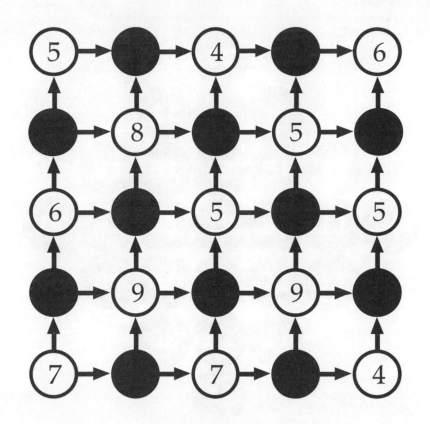

NUMBER PUZZLE 177

Move from the bottom left-hand corner to the top right-hand
corner following the arrows. Add the numbers on your route
together. If each black spot is worth 11,
how many times can you score 80?

ANSWER 180

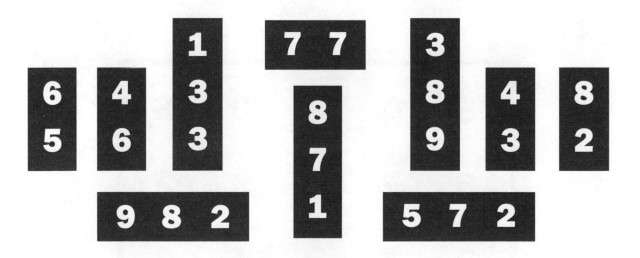

NUMBER PUZZLE 178

Place the tiles in the square to give some five-figure numbers.
When this has been done accurately the same
five numbers can be read both down and across.
How does the finished square look?

ANSWER 128

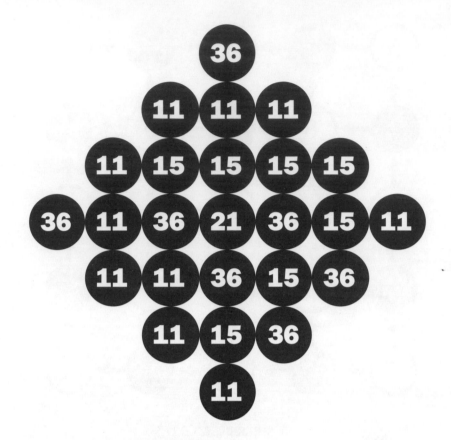

NUMBER PUZZLE 179

Start in the middle circle and move from circle to touching circle.
Collect the four numbers which will total 83. Once a route has
been found return to the middle circle and start again.
If a route can be found, which obeys the above rules but follows
both a clockwise and an anticlockwise path, it is treated as two
different routes.
How many different ways are there?

ANSWER 170

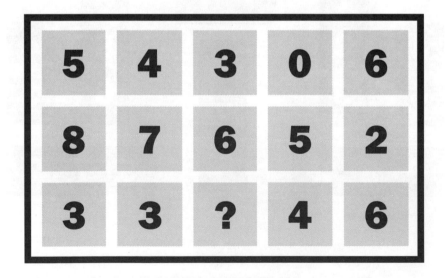

NUMBER PUZZLE 180

Which number should replace the question mark in the diagram?

ANSWER 118

NUMBER PUZZLE 181

You have five shots with each go to score 44. Aim at this target and work out how many different ways there are to make the score. Assume each shot scores and once five numbers have been used the same five cannot be used again in another order.
How many ways are there?

ANSWER 159

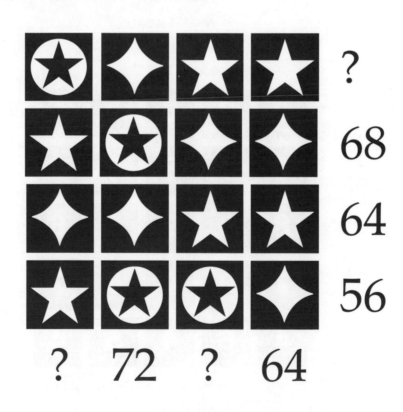

NUMBER PUZZLE 182

The contents of each box has a value. The total of the values is shown alongside a row or beneath a column. Which number should replace the question marks?

ANSWER 107

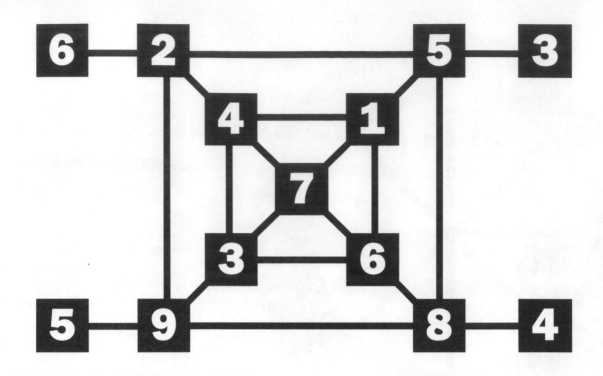

NUMBER PUZZLE 183

Start at any corner number and collect another four numbers by
following the paths shown. Add the five numbers together.
What is the lowest number you can score?

ANSWER 200

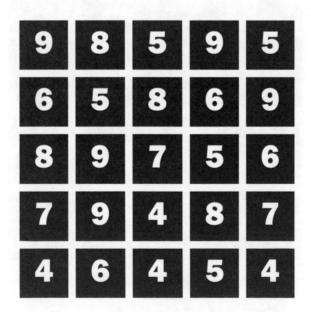

NUMBER PUZZLE 184

Move from square to adjacent square either vertically or horizontally. Begin at the bottom left-hand square and end at the top right-
hand square. Collect nine numbers and total them.
Which total can be scored only once?

ANSWER 148

A B C D E

A	B	C	D	E
9	3	6	7	9
8	3	5	6	8
7	3	4	5	
7	6	1	2	
6	5	1	2	6

NUMBER PUZZLE 185

There is a relationship between the columns of numbers in this
diagram. The letters above the grid are there to help you.
Which number should be placed in the empty squares?

ANSWER 189

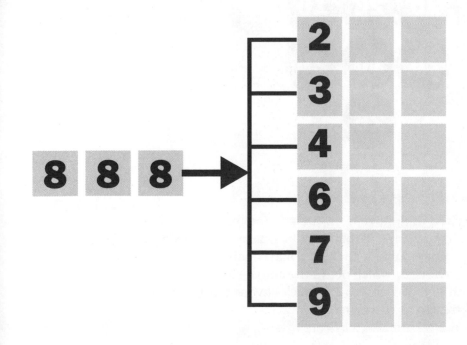

NUMBER PUZZLE 186

Place six three digit numbers of
100 plus at the end of 888 so that
six numbers of six digits are
produced. When each number is
divided by 77 six whole
numbers can be found. In this
case, the first numbers are given.
Which numbers should be
placed inthe grid?

ANSWER 137

12	3	12	3	10
6	10			2
	14		2	
			6	19
6		4	18	4

NUMBER PUZZLE 187

Each row, column and five-figure diagonal line in this diagram must total 40. Three different numbers must be used, as many times as necessary, to achieve this. What are the numbers?

ANSWER 179

NUMBER PUZZLE 188

Start in the middle circle and move from circle to touching circle. Collect the four numbers which will total 62. Once a route has been found return to the middle circle and start again. If a route can be found, which obeys the above rules but follows both a clockwise and an anticlockwise path, it is treated as two different routes. How many different ways are there?

ANSWER 127

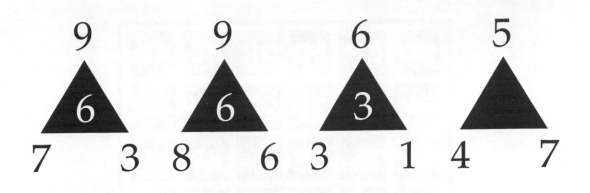

NUMBER PUZZLE 189

Which figure should be placed in the empty triangle?

ANSWER 117

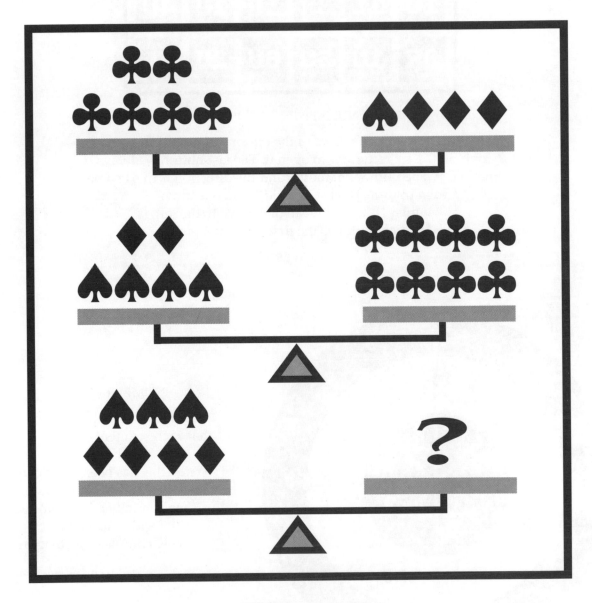

NUMBER PUZZLE 190

The top two scales are in perfect balance.
How many clubs will be needed to balance the bottom set?

ANSWER 169

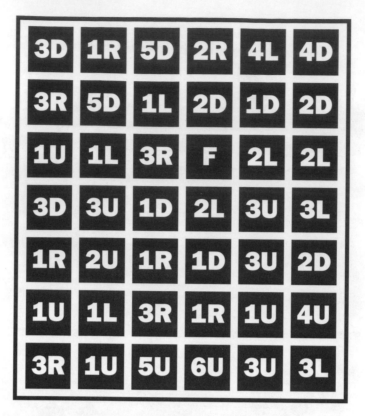

3D	1R	5D	2R	4L	4D
3R	5D	1L	2D	1D	2D
1U	1L	3R	F	2L	2L
3D	3U	1D	2L	3U	3L
1R	2U	1R	1D	3U	2D
1U	1L	3R	1R	1U	4U
3R	1U	5U	6U	3U	3L

NUMBER PUZZLE 191

Here is an unusual safe. Each of the buttons must be pressed once
only in the correct order to open it. The last button is always
marked F. The number of moves and the direction is marked on
each button. Thus 1U would mean one move up
whilst 1L would mean one move to the left.
Which button is the first you must press?

ANSWER 158

NUMBER PUZZLE 192

Complete the grid in such a way
that each segment of three numbers
totals the same.
When this has been done correctly
each of the three concentric circles of
eight numbers will produce
identical totals.
Now complete the diagram.

ANSWER 106

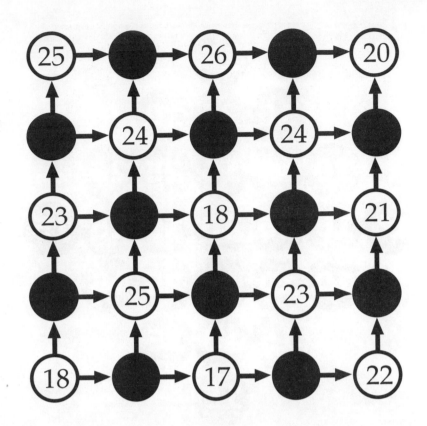

NUMBER PUZZLE 193

Move from the bottom left-hand corner to the top right-hand
corner following the arrows. Add the numbers on your route
together. If each black spot is worth minus 19,
how many times can you score 24?

ANSWER 199

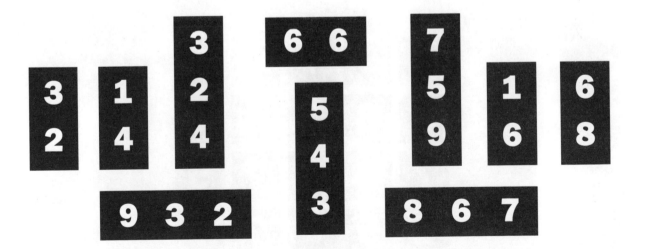

NUMBER PUZZLE 194

Place the tiles a square to give some five-figure numbers. When
this has been done accurately the same
five numbers can be read both down and across.
How does the finished square look?

ANSWER 147

NUMBER PUZZLE 195

Start in the middle circle and move from circle to touching circle.
Collect the four numbers which will total 90. Once a route has
been found return to the middle circle and start again.
If a route can be found, which obeys the above rules but follows
both a clockwise and an anticlockwise path, it is treated as two
different routes. How many different ways are there?

ANSWER 188

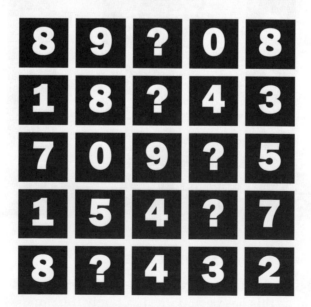

NUMBER PUZZLE 196

Which number should replace the question marks in the diagram?

ANSWER 136

NUMBER PUZZLE 197

You have three shots with each go to score 36. Aim at this target and work out how many different ways there are to make the score. Assume each shot scores and once three numbers have been used the same three cannot be used again in another order.
How many are there?

ANSWER 178

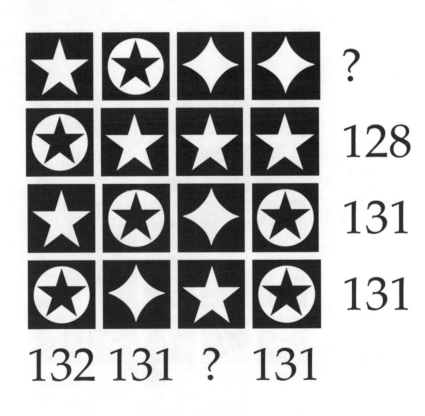

NUMBER PUZZLE 198

The contents of each box has a value. The total of the values is shown alongside a row or beneath a column. Which numbers should replace the question marks?

ANSWER 126

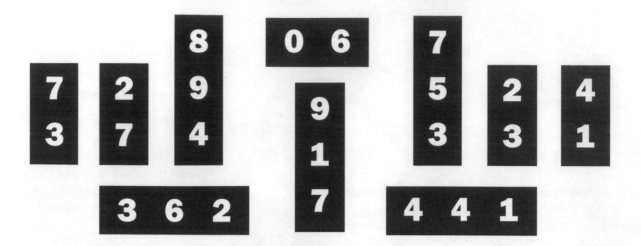

NUMBER PUZZLE 199

Place the tiles in a square to give some five-figure numbers.
When this has been done accurately the same
five numbers can be read both down and across.
How does the finished square look?

ANSWER 168

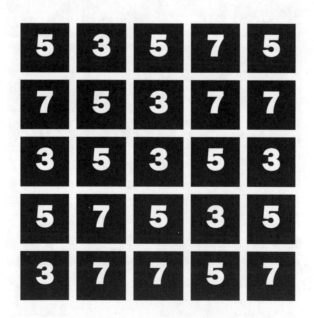

NUMBER PUZZLE 200

Move from square to adjacent square either vertically or
horizontally. Begin at the bottom left-hand square and end at the
top right-hand square. Collect nine numbers and total them.
How many different ways are there to total 39?

ANSWER 116

A B C D E

A	B	C	D	E
9	0	6	9	
8	1	6	9	7
7	2	6	9	8
7	1	5	8	
3	1	1	4	2

NUMBER PUZZLE 201

There is a relationship between the columns of numbers in this diagram. The letters above the grid are there to help you. Which number should be placed in the empty squares?

ANSWER 157

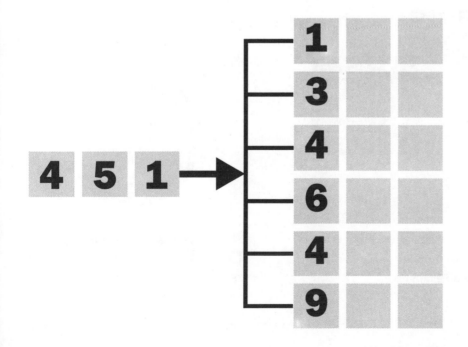

NUMBER PUZZLE 202

Place six three digit numbers of 100 plus at the end of 451 so that six numbers of six digits are produced. When each number is divided by 61 six whole numbers can be found. In this case, the first numbers are given. Which numbers should be placed inthe grid?

ANSWER 105

Answers

1   17.

2

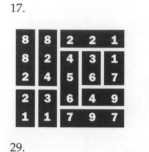

3   29.

4   10. The top number is multiplied by the bottom left-hand number and the total is divided by the bottom right-hand number.

5   1. The top row minus the bottom row gives the third row. The bottom row plus the second row gives the fourth row.

6   164
    295
    426
    557
    688
    819

7   Our answer is:

8   11 ways.

9   In two years time. The outer planet is 60 degrees in its orbit, the sun is in the middle and the inner planet is at 240 degrees.

10

11   8. The top row minus the bottom row gives the third row. The third row plus the second row gives the fourth row.

12   131
    264
    397
    663
    796
    929

13   Our answer is:

14   107 (values of symbols: ✧ = 18, ◆ = 30, ☆ = 29).

15   Once.

16

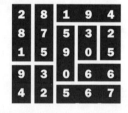

17   Once.

18   7. The top number is multiplied by the bottom left number and the bottom right number is taken away from this total to give the middle number.

19   5. 3rd row - top row = 5th row. 4th row + 5th row = 2nd.row.

20   162
    313
    464
    615
    766
    917

21

22   Three times.

23   4. The top number is added to the bottom left-hand number and the bottom right-hand number is subtracted.

24   6. The top row plus the second row gives the third row. The second row plus the fourth row gives the fifth row.

25   314
    425
    536
    647
    758
    869

26   Our answer is:

27   149 (values of symbols: ✧ = 35, ◆ = 42, ☆ = 37).

28   3 times.

29

30   3 ways.

31   Our answer is:

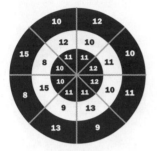

32   65 (values of symbols: ★ = 7, ♦ = 8, ✦ = 25, ☆ = 17).

33   In three and three-quarter years' time. The outer planet is 90 degrees in its orbit, the sun is in the middle and the inner planet is at 270 degrees.

34

3	9	7	8	6
9	8	2	4	3
7	2	5	1	1
8	4	1	9	9
6	3	1	9	0

35   Once.

36   3. The top number minus the bottom left-hand number is multiplied by the bottom right-hand number.

37   1. The second row plus the third row gives the top row. The third row plus the fourth row gives the bottom row.

38   431
542
653
764
875
986

39   Our answer is:

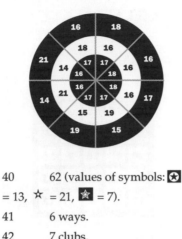

40   62 (values of symbols: ★ = 13, ✫ = 21, ✰ = 7).

41   6 ways.

42   7 clubs.

43   8. The middle row minus the bottom row equals the top row.

44   232
354
476
598
842
964

45   Our answer is:

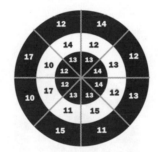

46   78 (values of symbols: ★ = 28, ✫ = 13, ✰ = 9).

47   In one and a half years' time. The outer planet is 90 degrees in its orbit, the sun is in the middle and the inner planet is at 270 degrees.

48

5	4	3	2	8
4	6	7	1	9
3	7	0	4	2
2	1	4	1	6
8	9	2	6	7

49   2 ways.

50   6. The bottom two numbers are added and taken from the top number.

51   5. Take the bottom row from the middle row to give the top row.

52   27 ways.

53   0, 1 and 4.

3	0	3	1	3
0	3	3	3	1
3	3	2	1	1
3	1	1	1	4
1	3	1	4	1

54   Four.

55   40.

56   4 spades.

57   10 ways.

58   2. A + B = D. A - B = C. D - C = E.

59   4U on the third row from the bottom.

60   204 (values of symbols: ☆ = 44, ♦ = 58, ✦ = 45).

61   10, 11, 23 and 31.

25	9	23	5	23
12	22	24	23	4
24	20	17	14	10
13	11	10	12	39
11	23	11	31	9

62   5 times.

63   14 ways.

64   4. A + B = D. A - E = C. D - C = E.

65   1L in the second column from the left one row from the bottom.

66   8 ways.

67   9, 17 and 18.

19	12	18	4	17
13	17	19	18	3
18	20	14	8	10
9	10	9	11	31
11	11	10	29	9

68   Four routes.

69   30.

70   7 clubs.

71   12 ways.

72   2. A + B = D. A - B = C. D - C = E.

73   58.

74   40 and once.

75   6 clubs.

76   7 ways.

77   4. A - B + 1 = D. D - 1 = C. D + B - 1 = E.

78   1L in the third column from the left on the third row from the bottom.

79   15 ways.

80   11, 12 and 21.

19	12	22	6	21
9	21	23	20	7
20	21	16	11	12
21	12	9	11	27
11	14	10	32	13

81   4 times.

82   37.

83   1U in the second column from the left on the second row.

84   7 ways.

85   9 and 17.

17	10	17	4	17
8	17	19	17	4
17	22	13	4	9
14	9	7	9	26
9	7	9	31	9

86   2 routes.

87   4 times.

88   4 diamonds.

89   7 ways.

90   3. A - B = D. C = D + 2. E = D - B.

91   1D fourth from the left on the top row.

92   11 ways.

93   27 and twice.

94   3. The top number minus the bottom left-hand number minus the   bottom right-hand number.

95   7 ways.

96   5. A - B = D. D + 2 = C. D - B = E.

97   3U on the bottom row.

98   21 ways.

99   11, 18 and 19.

19	13	21	3	19
14	19	20	18	4
20	23	15	7	10
11	12	10	11	31
11	8	9	36	11

100   One.

101   Twice.

102   5 clubs.

103   5 ways.

104   157 (values of symbols:  = 45, = 44, ☆ = 23).

105. 156
      339
      461
      644
      400
      949

106. Our answer is:

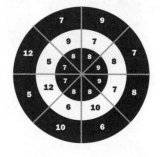

107. 52 (values of symbols: = 12, ☆ = 8, = 24).

108. 3 times.

109.

6	4	6	1	6
4	3	4	2	4
6	4	5	7	8
9	2	7	5	3
2	4	8	3	9

110. 60.

111. 8. The top number minus the bottom left–hand number multiplied by the right–hand number.

112. 8. 3rd row - top row = 5th row. 5th row + 4th row = 2nd row.

113. 233
     356
     479
     725
     848
     971

114. Our answer is:

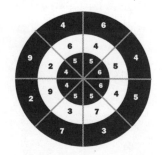

115. 217
     366
     515
     664
     813
     962

116. 2 times.

117. 7. The top number minus the bottom left–hand number multiplied by the right hand number.

118. 3. Top row + bottom row = middle row.

119. 279
     441
     522
     846
     765
     927

120. Our answer is:

121. 122 (values of symbols = 20, ☆ = 24, ★ = 42, ✩ = 36).

122. In 2 ¼ years time. The outer planet is 22.5 degrees in its orbit, the sun is in the middle and the inner planet is at 202.5 degrees.

123.

124. 2 ways.

125. 1, 3, and 4.

126. 126 at the side and 122 beneath (values of symbols: ☆ = 31, ◆ = 30, ✪ = 35).

127. 11 ways.

128.

129. 58 and 37.

130. 6. The top number multiplied by the bottom left–hand number minus the right–hand number.

131. 5. The top row plus the second row gives the third row. The second row plus the fourth gives the fifth row.

132. 145
224
461
777
856
935

133. Our answer is:

134. 53 (values of symbols: ☆ = 4, ✪ = 17, ✧ = 15).

135. 14 routes.

136. 6. 2nd row + 3rd row = top row. 3rd row + 4th row = 5th row.

137. 272
349
426
657
734
965

138. Our answer is:

139. 146 (values of symbols: ✧ = 38, ☆ = 37, ◆ = 34).

140. 90 and 92.

141.

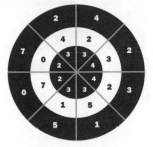

142. 4 ways.

143. 5. The top number is added to the bottom left–hand number and the bottom right–hand number is subtracted.

144. 3. The top row is the total of the 2nd and 3rd rows. The bottom row is the total of the 3rd and 4th rows.

145. 4 ½. The top number multiplied by the bottom left–hand number divided by the bottom right–hand number.

146. 5U on the second row from the bottom.

147.

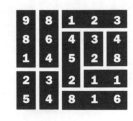

148. 54.

149. 4. The top number minus the two bottom numbers combined.

150. 2. The top row minus the bottom row gives the third row. The third row plus the second row gives the fourth row.

151. 195
415
635
745
855
965

152. Our answer is:

153. 47 (values of symbols ✧ = 6, ★ = 11, ☆ = 12, ◆ = 18).

154. 2 ways.

155.

156. In twelve and a half years time. The outer planet is 45 degrees in its orbit, the sun is in the middle and the inner planet is at 225 degrees.

157. 6. A + B = D. D – 3 = C. C + B = E.

158. 3U on the bottom row.

159. 34 ways.

160. 7, 8 and 15.

15	10	16	1	13
9	15	14	15	2
14	15	11	7	8
8	7	8	7	25
9	8	6	25	7

161. Once.

162. 2 ways.

163. 5 spades.

164. 9 ways.

165. A − B + 1 = D. D − 1 = C.
B + C = E.

166. 3D on the top row.

167. 1. A + B − 1 = D. D − 3 = C.
B + C = E

168.

8	9	4	4	1
9	1	7	2	7
4	7	5	3	3
4	2	3	0	6
1	7	3	6	2

169. 10 clubs.

170. 7 ways.

171. 7. A + B = D. D − 3 = C.
C + B = E.

172. 3R in the third column from
the left on the third row down.

173. 7 ways.

174. 8, 12, 13 and 14.

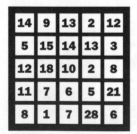

14	9	13	2	12
5	15	14	13	3
12	18	10	2	8
11	7	6	5	21
8	1	7	28	6

175. 19 ways.

176. 4 times.

177. 37 ways.

178. 9 ways.

179. 5, 8 and 11.

12	3	12	3	10
6	10	11	11	2
11	14	8	2	5
5	5	5	6	19
6	8	4	18	4

180. 8 times.

181. 6 times.

182. 9 clubs.

183. 7 ways.

184. 2. A − B = D. D + 2 = C.
D − B = E

185. 2R on the third row down in the
fourth column from the left.

186. 59 ways.

187. 3, 4 and 6.

4	2	4	1	4
2	4	4	4	1
4	4	3	2	2
3	2	2	2	6
2	3	2	6	2

188. 13 ways.

189. 7. A − B = C. C + 1 = D.
B + C = E.

190. 4U on the third row from the
bottom.

191. 21 ways.

192. 15, 17 and 24.

17	4	17	5	17
4	17	17	17	5
17	17	12	7	7
15	7	7	7	24
7	15	7	24	7

193. 8 times.

194. Once.

195. 3 diamonds.

196. 7 ways.

197. 7 clubs.

198. 9. A + B = D. D − 3 = C.
C + B = E..

199. Once.

200. 15.

201. 5 spades

202. 4 ways.